WILLIE ROBERTSON
and WILLIAM DOYLE

AMERICAN
HUNTER

HOW LEGENDARY
HUNTERS
SHAPED AMERICA

HOWARD BOOKS
AN IMPRINT OF SIMON & SCHUSTER
NEW YORK   NASHVILLE   LONDON   TORONTO   SYDNEY   NEW DELHI

Howard Books
An Imprint of Simon & Schuster, Inc.
1230 Avenue of the Americas
New York, NY 10020

First Howard Books hardcover edition October 2015

HOWARD and colophon are trademarks of Simon & Schuster, Inc.

For information about special discounts for bulk purchases, please contact Simon & Schuster Special Sales at 1-866-506-1949 or business@simonandschuster.com.

The Simon & Schuster Speakers Bureau can bring authors to your live event. For more information or to book an event, contact the Simon & Schuster Speakers Bureau at 1-866-248-3049 or visit our website at www.simonspeakers.com.

Interior design by Davina Mock-Maniscalco

Manufactured in the United States of America

10   9   8   7   6   5   4   3   2   1

Library of Congress Cataloging-in-Publication Data

Robertson, Willie, 1972–
  American hunter : how legendary hunters shaped America's history / Willie Robertson, William Doyle.—First Howard Books hardcover edition.
     pages cm
  Includes bibliographical references.
  1. Hunting—United States—History. 2. Hunters—United States—History.
  I. Doyle, William, 1957– II. Title.
  SK41.R575 2015
  639'.10973—dc23
                        2015027766

ISBN 978-1-5011-1133-4
ISBN 978-1-5011-1135-8 (ebook)

To the American Hunter

CONTENTS

*In the sweat of thy face shalt thou eat bread, till thou
return unto the ground; for out of it wast thou taken:
for dust thou art, and unto dust shalt thou return.*

—Genesis 3:19

CHAPTER 1

AN AMERICAN HUNTER IN THE FIELDS OF THE LORD

B e still!"

Phil whispers the command as he looks to the sky, gripping a twenty-gauge shotgun loaded with birdshot.

My brother Jase, Uncle Si, and I are crouched beside him, along with three of our buddies. We're hidden in a duck blind on our property in Northeast Louisiana near the Ouachita River. A duck flying overhead would never spot us. We're toting shotguns and wearing full duck-hunting camo. Our faces are smeared with black face paint and our ears are protected by plugs.

It's a good morning for duck hunting. The sun is burning off the mist and all is quiet except for the buzzing insects and the random sounds of the woods. It's nature in its purest form. Waiting, waiting, waiting—we do a lot of that.

We've had our morning coffee and biscuits that we cooked up in a little stove we keep in the back of the blind. Peggy Sue, our black Labrador retriever, stands inside the edge of the blind, every muscle straining to pounce into action.

My brother Jase blows on a duck call we made in our shop. Most people would just hear your basic "quack, quack, quack." But the call has been handcrafted with precision and sounds more like a duck than most ducks do. In duck language, it sounds like "Hey, how're you doing? Come on down here! This pond is a great place for ducks to hang out with other ducks and do fun duck things." Our hand-painted decoy ducks are bobbing in the pond, a friendly party invitation.

Beauty of the hunt, 2008 (Pat Hagan, US Fish & Wildlife Service)

One good ol' boy—a poet named Ogden Nash—said this about us duck-hunter types: "The hunter crouches in his blind, / 'Neath camouflage of every kind." That's us—six men versus a couple hundred juicy little birds.

Our guns are Mossbergs, made to our own specifications and under our own name. They're made in America, just the way we like. I prefer hunting with a twenty-gauge shotgun. It's lighter and you can swing it out a little more. It's not as powerful as some other guns and doesn't have as much range, but it's good for ducks and quail, even doves. It's easier to handle and gentler on my shoulder than the impact of ten-gauges and twelve-gauges, the really powerful guns.

When you're ready to fire, your brain makes complex calculations based on years of shooting and muscle memory. It's always different. You never know exactly where the animal will come from or how it will move. You've got to get out in front of those ducks and shoot ahead of their flight path so your shot hits them. Once you pull the trigger and fire, after your load travels thirty to forty yards, the bird drops.

That's with a twenty-gauge. The whole idea with a twenty-gauge is to get the ducks to come in as close as possible so you can get a good clean shot. A twelve-gauge will reach out farther and you can take perhaps a sixty- or seventy-yard shot; you've got the power and the load to make it there. With a smaller-caliber gun, you'd never take that shot; it wouldn't have enough range to reach its target.

I see a couple of big bass flipping around the pond and want to throw out a line and reel them in. But it would be risky to start fishing; I could totally lose the ducks.

It's September, early teal season in Louisiana, the time of year when enormous flocks of blue-winged ducks migrate during the Grand Passage from breeding grounds in Canada to below the border, as far south as Peru. Lots of them stop to take a break on our property. Like many other people, we are folks who look at ducks as a great food source. Ducks are eaten by many creatures, and we're just another one in line.

It's the time of year when Phil busts out nuggets of backwoods wisdom, like "The Grand Passage, it comes and then they go back. Most humans are totally unaware of it; they're oblivious to it. It's happening right above their head. But they never look up to see it. They miss a lot." He says this kind of thing at the beginning of every season. "The blue-wing's on the move, the Grand Passage has begun. Brush your blinds. Grab your gun. Let's go kill some ducks, boys." We're an old-school "farm to table" family, or, in this case, "sky to table."

We're an old-school "farm-to-table" family or, in this case, "sky-to-table."

The duck blind we're hiding in is one of nearly seventy duck blinds on our thousand-acre property. Ducks are a lot like airplanes; they're going to "light" (land) into the wind. So we position our blinds to capitalize on whatever direction the wind is blowing to get the ducks when they're coming down. We have blinds where you can only hunt well on a south wind or a north wind, and we have one big open water blind where you can only hunt well when it rains.

Pintail duck in flight at William L. Finley National Wildlife Refuge, Oregon (US Fish & Wildlife Service)

Ducks are all about vision and what they can see from the air. The approach they make will change based on the wind. Right at daylight is when you get big flurries of ducks flying around, and you've got to remember that not far away are other hunters pushing the ducks around. The ducks are just looking for safe water to settle in where no one's shooting at them!

Wood ducks are usually the first thing you see in the morning—they fly around like crazy. Teals are the same way. In fact, a teal hunt is typically over and done by eight a.m.; then the ducks quit flying. When he wakes up, the first thing a typical duck wants to do is eat, and he might go to a rice field. A lot of hunters will hunt in rice fields and do what you call "pass shooting," firing at the ducks as they pass over, from about fifty or sixty yards.

On the Robertson property we don't have rice fields, so we get ducks around nine a.m. who have already enjoyed their breakfast. They just want to find a spot to sit around all day and relax. We Robertsons have always liked to hunt ducks who have already eaten. When ducks are coming straight down into a patch of water, right before they land, they practically hover, or "break down." They sort of look like a falling balloon.

That's when you want to hit them, when they're slow and close. You're hidden, so they can't see you. But once you start firing, the ducks will reverse course, turn up the energy, and try to back out. They'll try to push right back up, which is difficult to do at any speed, so even though they're reacting to our gunfire, we still have a good chance to get them.

This is God's Grocery Store. The bounty of Earth is all around us. It's peaceful and beautiful out here; the fall foliage is green, orange, and gold against a blue sky.

Willie Robertson hunting (COPYRIGHT © WILLIE ROBERTSON)

You don't have to be crazy to be a duck hunter, but it does help. It's usually hot, sweaty, and humid during duck season, and you're constantly swatting at swarms of buzzing mosquitoes. Though the weather and mosquitoes are a nuisance, there's just one thing we Robertsons really fear out in the woods—snakes. Our biggest fear is the cottonmouth water moccasin. We always figure that they're probably slithering around not far off. There are a lot of snakes down here in Louisiana. If one gets in the duck blind, Uncle Si has a loaded pistol in his pants, ready to blow its head off. It's a little frightening when you're in a duck blind near the water and it's getting dark, because you know those cottonmouths are out there. So we keep flashlights on hand to make sure there aren't any snakes. We typically go in and try to clean the blinds out before the season starts. One year we went in a blind and killed nine cottonmouths. In the winter it's not as bad, although we've seen them all the way to December.

Most of the guys in the duck blind wear our trademark thick beards, myself included. The beard's original purpose was to protect us from the wind blowing in our faces. When you're out there in the woods hunting, facial hair helps keep you warm. That's why we first started with the beards, but now it's morphed into our signature look. Somebody once asked my dad, "How long have you been growing that beard?" He said, "I ain't growing it. It's doing that on its own."

Somebody once asked my dad, "How long have you been growing that beard?" He said, "I ain't growing it. It's doing that on its own."

I think 1988 was the last time Phil shaved his off. He lost a bet to a preacher, shaved his beard, and put on a suit. He said he'd never do it again. When Jase and I were younger and running the business, we thought we had to clean it up and put suits on to have business meetings with big companies. But about ten or twelve years ago I told Jase, "Forget that. Let's just go like we normally are." Sometimes in the heart of the summer, I look at people with their faces shaved and think it'd be nice, but once you get used to it, it's not as hot. Most guys say it gets itchy, but once you grow it out into a big man beard, the itching is gone.

My wife, Korie, actually likes my beard. In fact, the last time I shaved, she said, "I think you should grow it back." My youngest child has never seen me without it, and the last time I shaved, my older son started crying because he was used to the beard (that was a lot of years back—I don't think he'd cry about it now).

I haven't found a hat or sunglasses that'll cover up this look, so I get recognized quite often. It comes with the terrain, so I've gotten used to that too. I love it when little kids come up to me. I try to get down and hear what they have to say and ask them who their favorite person on the show is. Sometimes at the airport, if I'm trying to get through security and about to miss my flight, or I'm just running out to buy groceries, it gets a little old. But I tell everybody, when I quit being recognized, it means our show is probably not good anymore.

As far back as I can remember, we were always out there hunting as a family. Hunting and fishing were always part of the family business. Our family feels the same way about hunting that the baroness Ann Mallalieu felt: "Hunting is our heritage, it is our poetry, it is our art, it is our pleasure. It is where many of our best friendships are made, it is our community. It is our whole way of life."

Phil was a commercial fisherman before we started our hunting business. When I was a boy I helped sell his freshly caught fish at the market with my mom, Miss Kay. Even then I always tried to negotiate the price. But Phil always saved the best of the catch for our family and we ate a lot of fish growing up! We'd also share our fish with our church. We'd have a big fish fry at the church for people we were trying to convert. We'd feed forty or fifty people. Growing up in a family of hunters, we had a lot of shotguns on the property. We had .410 shotguns as kids, then moved up to twelve-gauge shotguns. I was about six when I learned to shoot a gun. "Hey, we're going hunting," Phil would say, and off we'd go. It was a normal childhood thing, not a big deal. We hunted every day we weren't in school. Phil didn't really treat us like children; he treated us more like little adults. We were good kids.

Phil was definitely old-school when it came to his sons hunting; it was an automatic thing. He always told us, "Hunting and being outdoors will keep a bunch of young men out of trouble. It's hard to do a lot of bad things when you're out sitting in a tree stand or a duck blind. It keeps you off the streets and you're doing something entertaining." The great South Carolina hunter and poet Archibald Rutledge sounded a little like Phil when he said:

> If more fathers were woodsmen, and would teach their sons to be likewise, most of the so-called father-and-son problems would vanish. . . . If a man brings up his sons to be hunters, they will never grow away from him. Rather the passing years will only bring them closer, with a thousand happy memories of the woods and fields.

That perfectly describes our family. Hunting is a huge reason why we're so close as a family.

Phil and my brothers Al and Jase taught me how to carry and handle guns, and they taught me firearms safety, too, so nobody accidentally got shot. We didn't shoot at targets, we shot at something real.

I have one particular memory of a dove hunt when I was about eight. Phil was not the kind of father who laid all of your gear out for you. He said, "You're in charge of getting your stuff together." I took along my little .410 single-barrel shotgun, one of the smallest-caliber shotguns there is. I realized I only had one shell. I said, "Dad, I only have one shell." He said, "Well, son, you've only got one shot. Better make it count." I thought, *Oh, crap! There's nothing like an all-day dove hunt when you've only got one shot!* I spent most of the day trailing Phil and picking up his birds; I was fascinated by the way he twirled their heads off. Finally, about three or four hours into the hunt, I had my best chance at a shot.

I took the shot. The dove fell. I was so proud. I looked over and Phil had shot at the same exact time that I had. It's a little unclear who exactly shot that bird, but I'm going to claim it. That one shot was successful!

Phil can remember the first time his father took him hunting. He was about eleven years old. He remembers aiming his shotgun and whispering to his dad, "What do I have?" The reply: "You got a green-winged teal and a pintail." He never forgot it. Today, he can take you to the very spot they were standing in and say, "Look, they were right there." He's been chasing ducks ever since.

BUT BACK TO THE DUCK BLIND, where the boys and I are waiting for the ducks. We wait and wait and wait. Jase blows away on the duck call. I peer across the horizon.

Suddenly, a flock of dozens of teals swoops in from the north, circling in a wide arc over the water. It's game time.

In the blind, Jase and Willie (COPYRIGHT © DUCK COMMANDER)

AN AMERICAN HUNTER IN THE FIELDS OF THE LORD

"Big bunch, big bunch," whispers Phil, "right over there!" We tighten our grips on our guns and wait for the final word. "Coming down the lane, coming toward us. Here they come . . ."

They come closer, closer, then level off in a horizontal pass right in front of the blind as they prepare to light on the water. There are so many of them and they're so close, it sounds like a jumbo jet passing.

"Kill 'em," says Phil firmly.

In an instant, six men and six guns pop out of the brush and open fire. "Shoot low," says Phil.

The roar of blasting gunfire echoes hard and loud off the water. It's a war zone. It looks like a wartime guerilla ambush. Bursts of shot catch ducks in midflight, one after the other, instantly killing most of them and sending them down in hard splashes to the water. Some spin, others drop straight down, motionless. The dog is so excited she can barely stand it, but she knows to stay put until the shooting stops.

I knock down two ducks escaping overhead who are flying close together, and one even slams into the duck blind, within arm's reach. We're shooting real good, each man bringing down different ducks. The sky is filled with floating feathers and it looks kind of like a ticker-tape parade.

"Cut him, Jase," says Phil, gesturing toward an escaping bird. "Hit that drake!" Jase knocks him down with one shot.

Food falls from the sky. One of our buddies chuckles, "It's raining feathers, it's raining ducks!" Ten, twenty birds drop to the ground and the count keeps going. Spent shotgun shell casings drift in the water.

"Now we're cooking with peanut oil!" shouts Uncle Si after a while. "We've done killed more than twenty ducks in twenty minutes!"

"Now we're cooking with peanut oil!" shouts Uncle Si after a while. "We've done killed more than twenty ducks in twenty minutes!"

Eventually, the shots subside. There's a lot of paranoia in a duck blind if things go wrong. On those days, Uncle Si will grumble, "You've got to use more face paint! The light reflected off your face and the ducks flared off! Gotta put face paint on the beards. Put more brush in the back of the blind. The dog's wagging her tail too much and bumping the blind!" But this is not one of those days. This is one of the best days a duck hunter can have. When everything lines up and practically all of the shootable ducks fall from our shots, it's called a rainout. The Robertsons have made an art form of the rainout.

My brother Jase, an excellent shot, is jubilant and says, "I made a hundred-yard shot, I know that! I really think there's something to those hand-painted decoys." Phil, in the far left spot in the blind, is satisfied and says, "I was knocking them down over here."

Uncle Si, as usual, claims incredible feats of marksmanship: "Well, I don't know about you boys, but I was four for four! What can I say? It was just like jungle fighting in Vietnam. You see how tight my pattern was?"

Soon, we're snacking on ducks we've cooked on our little stove in the duck blind, flavored with Italian dressing. "That tastes pretty dang good," someone says. "That's a gumbo duck there, boys!" If you've never tasted fresh killed-and-grilled duck right under an open sky, you haven't lived.

At the end of the day, we pile the ducks into a boat and go back home. Everybody in the family pitches in to prepare the food for the dinner table. It's like an assembly line; everyone has a job to do. After Jase and I pick off the feathers, someone lightly singes the hair and excess feathers off the duck over a fire. Then Miss Kay takes over the cooking and dressing, and she's helped by whichever family members are at hand. If she's making gumbo, we'll help her with the chopping.

After we clean and cook the birds, we all sit down to eat at the dinner table after saying a prayer. Then we tell stories about the hunt.

When I was growing up we only had three channels on the TV and no video games, so being out in the woods and telling stories about our adventures was what we did. We were very poor, so we were our own entertainment, and it was at the dinner table that we learned to tell stories. If you were a kid at our house and were telling a story, it had better be a good one, because you were holding the audience's attention. I really think that's how our charismatic personalities were shaped.

I also think that practice helped us with storytelling in our TV shows. If you had a story to tell, you had to make it big or it would be overshadowed by someone else's!

We spent the whole day with family and friends, and we succeeded in doing what we went out to do—get a dozen ducks on the dinner table so we'd have the food we needed and sit down together with our family.

For me, that's a good day at the office.

———

I AM AN AMERICAN HUNTER.

Hunting is my heritage, my business, and my life. It is my passion, my exercise, my relaxation, my profession, and my destiny. It is the foundation of my family's life together.

> **I hunt to eat. I hunt to enjoy life with my family and friends. And I hunt to honor God.**

I hunt to eat. I hunt to enjoy life with my family and friends. And I hunt to honor God. I will be a hunter until the day the Good Lord takes me home.

In my life, I focus on four main things: faith, family, ducks, and deer. As with all good things in life, it begins with God.

I consider America to be one of the greatest gifts God ever gave mankind. Since the days of Native American dominion, and in the centuries since the arrival of European settlers through today, America has been a rich natural paradise of wild game and fish, forests and mountains teeming with life, rushing waters, natural crops, wide-open spaces, and indescribable beauty.

I have spent many years roaming the Lord's American fields, hunting His game, stalking through His forests and wetlands, forging through His hills and streams. Barely a moment goes by when I am not totally in awe of what an incredible gift from God America is. Few other lands in the world are as blessed as we are.

Like most of the people in my family, I love pretty much anything to do with the outdoors. I love walking in the woods; sucking in fresh, clean air; camping out under the stars (all right, I'll confess, sometimes I've been known to camp in an RV instead of a tent), or tearing around my backyard in an ATV. I love playing a round of golf or waterskiing with my wife and kids. But hunting brings me so close to nature in its purest form that it's really become a passion for me.

God put us on Earth for many reasons—to help our fellow man, to love one another, and to raise our children on the path of righteousness.

And God put us on Earth to hunt. I truly believe it. On this, the Bible is clear. In a number of biblical passages, we are encouraged to hunt and fish, to enjoy the bountiful gifts of Creation and be nourished by them.

In Genesis 9:1–3, God commands Noah and his sons:

Be fruitful, and multiply, and replenish the earth. And the fear of you and the dread of you shall be upon every beast of the earth, and upon every fowl of the air, upon all that moveth upon the earth, and upon all the fishes of the sea; into your hand are they delivered. Every moving thing that liveth shall be meat for you; even as the green herb have I given you all things.

Are you as moved and inspired by this gift as I am? Whenever I read these words, I am struck with a sense of responsibility, humility, and wonder. Like so much in the Bible, the more you think about it, the more the verses reach you on multiple, deep, meaningful levels.

God commands us to "be fruitful and multiply," but He adds the instruction to "replenish the earth." Besides telling us to replenish the earth, I believe He also wants us to renew our world by treating it with love and care, out of obedience and respect for Him and for the benefit of future generations. He is telling us to be responsible stewards of Earth, which is something all good hunters take very seriously as a covenant to be cherished. After all, hunters were among the first and strongest American conservationists, and remain so today.

The former president of the Boone and Crockett Club Lowell Baier said that the ones "who know well the game they hunt . . . yearn for the opportunity to find peace, tranquility, and solitude in nature and fellowship in camp. They become conservationists as a natural outgrowth of their appreciation for their sport."

And finally, God tells us to establish provenance over "every moving thing" on the planet, all the beasts, birds, and fish, because "into your hand are they delivered." In other words, the bounty of life is God's gift to us. As Phil once put it, "We've got orders from headquarters. If he walks, crawls, flies, or swims, whack him, stack him, and eat him." He added, "Where there's design, there is a designer. We were designed to kill ducks."

The idea of hunting and fishing as ways of nourishing humanity echoes throughout the Bible. In Genesis 27:3–4, Isaac, the son of Abraham, believing he has not much longer to live, summons his own son Esau and commands him, "Now therefore take, I pray thee, thy weapons, thy quiver and thy bow, and go out to the field, and take me some venison;

> The idea of hunting and fishing as ways of nourishing humanity echoes throughout the Bible.

And make me savoury meat, such as I love, and bring it to me, that I may eat; that my soul may bless thee before I die."

In Acts 10:10–16, Simon Peter prays so hard that he falls into a trance. Then, the Bible relates, he "saw heaven opened, and a certain vessel descending upon him, as it had been a great sheet knit at the four corners, and let down to the earth: Wherein were all manner of fourfooted beasts of the earth, and wild beasts, and creeping things, and fowls of the air. And there came a voice to him, Rise, Peter; kill, and eat. But Peter said, Not so, Lord; for I have never eaten any thing that is common or unclean. And the voice spake unto him again the second time, What God hath cleansed, that call not thou common. This was done thrice: and the vessel was received up again into heaven." .

It is a simple Bible principle that reflects the reality of human life and survival for thousands of years: *rise, kill, and eat.*

Jesus Christ himself was a fishing enthusiast, and it wasn't just when he multiplied the loaves and fishes to feed the multitude. Two of Jesus' great miracles revolved around catching fish. In Luke 5:1–11, early in Jesus' ministry, after preaching the word of God to a crowd from a boat on the Sea of Galilee, he said to Simon Peter the fisherman, "Launch out into the deep, and let down your nets for a draught." Simon replied, "Master, we have toiled all the night, and have taken nothing: nevertheless at thy word I will let down the net." In a flash, so many fish swarmed toward the boat that the net broke. Another fishing boat raced over to help out, and soon both boats were sinking from the weight of so many fish. The Bible says the fishermen were "astonished" at the quantity of fish they caught. Instantly, Simon Peter became a disciple of Jesus, along with two of his fisherman partners, James and John, sons of Zebedee. Jesus assured Simon Peter, "Fear not; from henceforth thou shalt catch men."

Years later, one evening after the Resurrection of Jesus, according to the Gospel of John 21:1–14, seven of his grieving disciples decided to go fishing and caught nothing. Early on the following morning, Jesus appeared on the shore and called out,

"Children, have ye any meat?" The disciples, not recognizing their Lord, said no. Jesus called out, "Cast the net on the right side of the ship, and ye shall find." Sure enough, no less than 153 fish swam into their net and were hauled aboard. "It is the Lord," exclaimed one of the disciples, who was shocked to recognize the face of Jesus, whom they had witnessed dying days before. At this, an ecstatic Simon Peter jumped into the water to greet Jesus on the shore. Again, the setting for this epic scene of Christianity was catching fish.

At the same time, the Bible contains several passages forbidding cruelty to animals, which is a command all good hunters take most seriously. As Proverbs 12:10 says, "A righteous man regardeth the life of his beast," which to me means two things: not allowing animals to suffer needlessly and eating what you kill. In my family, we make a point of bringing the results of our hunting to our dinner table, or to someone else's dinner table.

AMERICA WAS CREATED IN LARGE part by hunters, fishers, trappers, and mountain men. As Teddy Roosevelt put it, "The virility, clear-sighted common sense and resourcefulness of the American people is due to the fact that we have been a nation of hunters and frequenters of the forest, plains, and waters."

It's about time we thanked them, by telling their incredible stories of skill, courage, survival, and—let's face it—downright bodaciousness. That's why my friend William Doyle and I put together this book for you. We wrote it for folks who love hunting, sport shooting, and wide-open spaces, and for folks who love American history. It's our history of hunting in America, but you can think of it as a collection of true stories you'll tell around the campfire after a long day's hunt.

To gather these stories together, we took a trip into the collections of some of the most amazing places in America, some of which you may not have seen for yourself: The Smithsonian Gun Room, which is kind of like a secret temple of some of the rarest and most precious firearms in American history, including a musket belonging to Thomas Jefferson. It's the ultimate "gun room" on Earth. The Buffalo Bill Center of the West in Cody, Wyoming, which is five museums in one: the Plains Indian Museum, the Whitney Western Art Museum, the Cody Firearms Museum, the Draper Natural History Museum, and, of course, a museum dedicated to old Buffalo Bill himself. The National Archives near Washington, DC, which is home to an incredible collection of historical hunting documents, diaries, and photos. The NRA's National Firearms Museum in Virginia and Sporting Arms Museum in Missouri. The New York Public Library, whose treasures include an antique original copy of a biography of Daniel Boone published in 1859 and an edition of the autobiography of Davy Crockett from 1903, both discovered in the rare books collection of the library.

So throw some meat on the grill, pop open a cold soda, and gather round the fire, boys and girls.

Every word I'm about to tell you is true, as far as I can tell.

Come with me on a trip back to our roots, to the days when America was young, when beasts roamed the land, and mankind battled with nature and prayed to the Lord for deliverance.

Come with me into the heart of the American hunter.

The Archer is awake!
The Swan is flying!
Gold against blue
An Arrow is lying.
There is hunting in heaven—
Sleep safe till tomorrow.

—William Carlos Williams, "Peace on Earth"

CHAPTER 2

A HUNTER'S PARADISE

They could hardly believe their eyes.

They had stepped into a hunter's paradise.

The first Europeans to land in America were stunned by the mind-boggling numbers and variety of animals they found in the forests, fields, streams, and mountains of the vast New World.

One member of Hernando de Soto's expedition through Florida and the American Southeast, which began in 1539, reported that he saw bears, wolves, deer, cats, rabbits, dogs, cranes, ducks, pigeons, thrushes, sparrows, blackbirds, hawks, goshawks, and falcons. He could barely keep track of all the different creatures as he scribbled in his journal.

When English captain Henry Hudson sailed into what is now New York Bay in 1609 on a commercial mission for the Dutch

East India Company, he and his men were spellbound by throngs of wood ducks, mallards, great blue herons, and songbirds, as well as the owls, grouses, hens, nighthawks, pelicans, whitetail deer, beavers, muskrats, minks, otters, squirrels, foxes, wolves, rabbits, raccoons, and pumas that filled in the woods, fields, and sky.

A local Native American chief who greeted Hudson ordered his braves to rustle up some game to give to the visitors as a welcome-to-the-neighborhood gift. Off they went into the woods. Hudson and his boys were shocked to see them come back in no time at all, their arms filled with a wide assortment of tasty birds and critters.

Hudson reported back to his Dutch bosses, in effect, *Get over there, now! There's a ton of money to be made!* He convinced them that Manhattan was a perfect place to launch a fur-trading operation, and by 1626 a typical Dutch ship crossing the Atlantic from the new Dutch post of New Amsterdam was stuffed with a cargo of eight hundred otter skins and seven thousand beaver skins.

In Massachusetts in the 1600s, you could bump into a flock of nearly one thousand wild turkeys wandering around the woods. On the Virginia coast, an English settler was overjoyed to count a total of twenty-eight species of animals and eighty-six different birds. Beyond the western horizon were buffaloes, elks, deer, antelopes, moose, wolves, foxes, beavers, bears, porcupines, muskrats, panthers, pumas, cougars, bobcats, and coyotes.

1-10 White tailed Deer
11-12 Elk
13-15 Mule Deer
16 Moose

22.

Deer, elk, and moose (Bob Hines, US Fish & Wildlife Service)

The smart Europeans quickly figured out that the key to tapping the infinite hunting potential of the New World was to gain the knowledge of the Native Americans, who had been American hunters for more than ten thousand years.

The Native Americans were master trappers, hunters, and fishermen, and were themselves creatures of the forests, plains, hills, and streams. They got not only most of their food and clothing from wild animals, but also much of life's other necessities.

Native Americans got not only most of their food and clothing from wild animals, but also much of life's other necessities.

Starting in boyhood, young Native American men learned to trap, stalk, and kill game; whole native communities got together to cooperate in mass hunts and animal drives. The Native Americans used animal skins for clothes, shelter, bowstrings, and tools. Antlers were cut into arrow and spear tips, and bones were whipped into knives, spoons, combs, fishhooks, digging tools, and even sewing needles.

For woodland tribes in the East, the vast population of whitetail deer was a one-stop supermarket of useful items, and every piece of the animal was used. The deer offered meat for cooking, hides to be transformed into durable weather-resistant clothing and satchels, skulls that could be used as bowls or spoons, shoulder blades that could be used as scraping tools, sinews to serve as sewing threads, and brains, which were used for tanning leather.

The Native Americans had countless ways of dispatching animals. In the forests, they perfected the art of blending into the scenery, freezing perfectly still for long periods, and gliding through the woods silently on moccasined feet. Sometimes, when they came face-to-face with a larger animal, they would stare it down or gently speak to it to "psych it out." The Native Americans' favorite handheld weapons were throwing spears for short-range action; stone clubs used for smacking a wounded deer or bear in the head, the coup de grace; and the famous bow and arrow, made from specially chosen wood such as hickory, hemlock, or white oak. Bowstrings were fashioned from rawhide.

Elk hunt (ALFRED JACOB MILLER, WALTERS ART MUSEUM)

When the Sioux nation had wide access to horses in the 1700s and 1800s, a favorite weapon for killing buffaloes was the mounted hunting lance. Made of wood and tipped with a long steel or iron tip, the lance measured over eight feet long and was used for thrusting, not throwing. A Native American on horseback would ride up next to the target, repeatedly rest the tip on the target's back to let it get accustomed to the sensation, then quickly thrust it down through the buffalo's vital organs for an instant kill. Also during this period, Native Americans obtained firearms like smoothbore "trade guns," which were preferred over rifles since they were lighter to carry and faster to reload.

The Iroquois and Menominee built snare traps of vines attached to trees that grabbed an animal's legs and yanked it up in the air in a noose. On the plains, tribes dressed up as buffaloes to slowly sneak up on unsuspecting herds and pick off the outliers. Likewise, the Pamunkey of the Powhatan Confederacy dressed up in full deerskin, crept along on all fours, then fired lightning-fast arrows at their targets from close range. Some braves were so skilled at shooting they could fill the air with multiple arrows at once.

The Eastern Native Americans used a ten-foot-long, dart-firing blowgun to bag small game. In California, a Native American hunter, breathing through a reed, would float underwater beneath ducks bobbing on streams, grab one, and pull it underwater. And just like our family, Native American hunters used hand-carved duck decoys to lure their prey into shooting range—in this case, bow-and-arrow style.

To bag big animals like bears, buffaloes, and elks, Native Americans would stalk and chase a target until it was exhausted, then move in for the kill, or use ingenious methods of trapping. The "baited pit" was a downward-sloping earthen trap cut into the ground with sides that sloped inward, preventing the animal from escaping. The "deadfall" was a forest trap made of heavy logs placed above a baited stick. When an animal tugged on the stick, the logs slammed down and killed it. In the "ring hunt," Native Americans would manipulate columns of grass fires to guide deer into the kill zone, a dangerous tactic that could trigger out-of-control fires that could devastate wide areas. An easier tactic was to simply find a bear in a tree, set the tree on fire, and kill the bear when it came down.

In some Eastern tribes, the Native Americans apologized to a bear before killing it, explaining, in effect, "I'm sorry I have to do this, but I need you for food and clothing!" For forest Native Americans in the American Northeast, like the Mohawks, a perfect meal might be slices of roasted venison dipped in a bear-fat-and-maple-sugar sauce.

For Plains Indians, the buffalo was considered a powerful, sacred animal, and they often prayed to the animals before killing them.

But there was one big animal that occupied the center of the religious and food universe for many Plains Indians tribes, like the Blackfeet, Cheyenne, Sioux, and Comanche. It was the buffalo, or technically, the bison. For

Plains Indians, the buffalo was considered a powerful, sacred animal, and they often prayed to the animals before killing them.

The Plains buffalo was a six-foot-tall, ten-foot-long, two-thousand-pound behemoth that offered meat, clothing, tools, and sacred religious meaning for the Native Americans. There were perhaps fifty million of them roaming the plains when the white man arrived in North America, in vast herds that may have represented the biggest formations of large animals in world history. They thrived in one-hundred-ten-degree summers and minus-fifty-degree winters, and they could run at thirty miles an hour and keep running for miles.

A buffalo bull's head was so big and its neck muscles so powerful that he could chuck a wolf thirty feet in the air with one head-snap. Its skull was so thick it was nearly bulletproof. "The bison is the chief of all animals and represents the earth, the totality of all that is," said Black Elk, a nineteenth-century Oglala Sioux. "It is the feminine, creating earth principle which gives rise to all living things."

In the eastern foothills of the Rocky Mountains, in what is now Wyoming and Montana, Native Americans used the "buffalo jump" method of killing the animal, where whole communities would cooperate in carefully stalking and guiding masses of the animals toward a steep cliff. Teams of Native Americans would pitch in to chase and steer the beasts over the precipice, then butcher the animals and fashion the carcasses into a variety of useful items. Several hundred buffaloes could be killed this way, creating tens of thousands of pounds of usable meat. Another technique was the "*piskin*" method, when tribes would surround and herd buffaloes into a mile-long man-made corral of fallen trees and boulders, then kill the animals.

A tribe would chow down on fresh meat and blood for days after a big kill. Buffalo meat provided delicious, protein-rich meals. Raw buffalo liver and kidney were especially nutritious, and buffalo fetuses and tongues were considered choice cuts. Every possible piece of the animal was eaten, including the blood, milk, marrow, testicles, nipples, and even the nose gristle.

Native American "buffalo jump" (ALFRED JACOB MILLER, WALTERS ART MUSEUM)

To the Plains Indians, the buffalo was a "general store" of other materials that could be used in religious ceremonies and in everyday life, including tents, robes, food, bone tools, utensils, and even fuel for fires. The horns provided spoon ladles. The hides were fashioned into shields, snowshoes, ropes, tepee covers, and pouches. The bladder was turned into a tobacco pouch. Buffalo blood was dabbed on arrows to increase penetration. The dung, or buffalo chips, was used as cooking fuel. Even the tail was put to good use—as a flyswatter. "Everything the Kiowa had came from the buffalo," said one tribeswoman, Old Lady Horse. "The buffalo were the life of the Kiowa. Most of all, the buffalo was part of the Kiowa religion." A Plains Indian named Lame Deer explained that the natives absorbed the buffalo's flesh and blood until it became their own flesh and blood, to the point where "it was hard to say where the animal ended and the man began."

One day in 1872, the Pawnee of the central plains did something unusual: they invited a white man to participate in a traditional mass buffalo hunt. Their guest, an outdoors-loving New York City man named George Grinnell, caught a westbound train out of Grand Central Terminal, mounted a horse, and became an honorary Native American hunter for ten days. The scenes he witnessed give us an extremely rare glimpse of what it was like to see a great buffalo hunt in action.

Native Americans on a buffalo hunt (LIBRARY OF CONGRESS)

Grinnell was amazed by the scale and pageantry of the hunt. "The scene that we now beheld was such as might have been witnessed here a hundred years ago," he wrote. "It is one that can never be seen again. Here were eight hundred warriors, stark naked, and mounted on naked animals. A strip of rawhide, or a lariat, knotted about the lower jaw, was all their horses' furniture. Among all these men there was not a gun nor a pistol, nor any indication that they had ever met with the white men."

Four thousand Pawnee men, women, and children were on the move across Nebraska, the entire Pawnee nation, led by eight hundred magnificent, naked Native American hunters on horseback, their long black hair flowing in the wind. This one summer hunt had to fill up the tribe's supply of dried meat for the next six months, so it was organized meticulously, with little room for error. "Bison-calling" ceremonies were held by priests and medicine men, complete with songs, dances, and prayers. As a priest moved his hand over hunting tools placed in a line of buffalo skulls, he chanted, "Father, you are the Ruler—We are poor—Take pity on us—Send us plenty of buffalo, plenty of fat cows—Father, we are your children—help the people—send us plenty of meat, so that we may be strong and our bodies may increase and our flesh grow hard—Father, you see us, listen."

This one summer hunt had to fill up the tribe's supply of dried meat for the next six months.

"Side by side, at the head of the column, walk eight men who carry the buffalo staves," he reported. "These are slender spruce poles, like a short lodge-pole, wrapped with blue and red cloth, and elaborately ornamented with bead work, and with the feathers of hawks, and of the war eagle. These sticks are carried by men selected by the chiefs and doctors in private council, and are religiously guarded. Upon the care of these emblems, and the respect paid to them, depends, in a great measure, the success of the hunt. While borne before the moving column, no one is permitted to cross the line of march in front of them." Behind them came the head chief and a dozen subchiefs, all mounted on superb horses. Behind them came the rest of the tribe, including women, young girls, and children, "a fantastically mingled multitude, marching without any appearance of order."

A "police force" of twenty-four experienced Native American warriors was given the job of managing and controlling the whole operation. Reporting to the tribal chiefs, they plotted out the day's march and the night's camping. They picked the scouts who traveled ahead of the tribe to spy on the buffaloes and spot the approaches for the attack. And if anybody messed up and did something that jeopardized the success of the hunt, these warriors had absolute authority to enforce brutal discipline, including beatings, on the offender. If someone stepped out of line—*wham*, he was laid flat on the ground with a well-placed smack from a club.

"*Halt!*" the scouts signaled.

They were atop a high bluff; they had spotted the buffaloes.

The wide valley below was blackened with over a thousand buffaloes, sleeping, lounging, and munching on grass. It was the perfect place to stage a "surround," and the mounted hunters quietly glided downhill to flank and envelop the targets in a circular trap and mounted chase.

Suddenly, some of the closest buffaloes sensed the approaching Native Americans and gazed at them in bewilderment. Instantly, a thousand buffaloes were on their feet, tails in the air, stampeding away from the hunters.

The senior Pawnee warrior shouted, "*Loo´-ah!*"

It was the order to charge. "Like an arrow from a bow each horse darted forward," reported Grinnell. "Each rider hoped to be the first to reach the top of the opposite ridge, and to turn the buffalo back into the valley, so that the surround might be completely successful. How swift those little ponies were, and how admirably the Indians managed to get out of them all their speed!"

Then the hunting began, and while it may have looked like a bloody, chaotic melee, it was actually performed with methodical precision. In a successful surround operation, the Native Americans constantly circled the buffalo herd in an ever-tightening noose, exhausting the animals in the process. A team of a hundred hunters could kill up to five hundred buffaloes in an hour. "The report of firearms was seldom heard," wrote Grinnell. "Most of the Indians hunted with the primitive weapon of their forefathers—the bow and arrow. For buffalo running an arrow is nearly as effective as lead. The power of the bow in expert hands is tremendous. Riding within half a dozen yards of the victim's side, the practiced bowman will drive the dart so far through the body of the buffalo that its shaft may project a foot or more from the opposite side—sometimes indeed may pass quite through." In the hands of a skilled shooter, the bow and arrow were incredibly fast and effective. Grinnell watched one Native American fire six arrows faster and more accurately than a six-barreled revolver.

At full speed, while the Native American hunter's hands were working the bow and arrow, he would lean down on his mount and fire an arrow from under the buffalo's neck *while steering his horse, with his legs only!* These maneuvers required lots of skill—and sheer guts. At any moment, a buffalo could lower his head and knock over and gore a hunter and his horse.

Grinnell watched the hunt go on for hours as fallen buffaloes littered the field. "It was sad to see so much death," thought Grinnell, "but the people must have food, and none of this meat would be wasted." Cooking fires flickered across the landscape as ribs were roasted, calves' heads were baked, and livers and hearts were eaten raw. The Pawnee ate, smoked, sang, and danced the night away.

It was the last mass buffalo hunt the Pawnee ever staged. The following year, the tribe imploded under pressure from Sioux attacks and the great collapse of the American buffalo herds. One thing above all else was responsible for both the fall of Native America as a hunting force and the rise of European and white settlers as American hunters. It was the American long rifle and its successors. And no man better symbolized the dawn of this new weapon, and the new breed of American hunter, than Daniel Boone.

*The West would never have been settled
save for the fierce courage and the eager desire
to brave danger so characteristic
of the stalwart backwoodsman.*
—Theodore Roosevelt, *The Winning of the West*

*When Daniel Boone goes by, at night,
The phantom deer arise
And all lost, wild America
Is burning in their eyes.*
—Rosemary and Stephen Vincent Benét, *A Book of Americans*

CHAPTER 3

THE LONG
HUNTERS

There I was, up in a tree.

I could hear a deer breathing somewhere close by, and I braced myself, waiting for him to come into view. My heart pounded in the cool morning air.

I heard twigs snap and grass rustle as the whitetail buck came closer.

In my arms I cradled a long piece of sculpted wood and iron, and it almost seemed as if I were channeling the spirit of the greatest early American hunter of them all, Daniel Boone.

I was on a deer hunt in northern Louisiana, and my weapon was an old-fashioned, single-shot, flintlock, muzzle-loading American long rifle.

Deer (LIBRARY OF CONGRESS)

I think there's an original pioneer man or pioneer woman inside all of us, and on this day I wanted to travel back in history, get in touch with my inner mountain man, and see what it felt like to hunt with the kind of weapon the original American hunters and trappers had to use when the country was mostly wilderness.

I was gripping a lightweight, long-barreled, black-powder muzzle-loader, not too far from the kind of rifle that Daniel Boone used on the frontier in the 1700s or George Washington's frontier rifle squads used in the Revolutionary War. No fancy scopes, high-tech ammo, or space-age designs.

In Louisiana, the muzzle-loading season for deer starts a week before the regular season, and it gives hunters a chance to try their skill at a very special form of shooting. Today, over a million hunters in the United States use muzzle-loaders, and it's easy to see why. A muzzle-loader brings you much closer to the animal, as close as fifty yards or so, versus the over two hundred yards you can hit a deer from using a cutting-edge modern weapon and scope. Plus black-powder rifles can kill an animal quickly and humanely.

Many hunters use percussion models, as a flintlock can misfire more often and take a while to reload. Dating back to the early 1800s, the percussion rifle uses a little cap that fits over a nipple outside the breech. You squeeze the trigger, a hammer hits the cap, and a spark flies

> I wanted to travel back in history, get in touch with my inner mountain man, and see what it felt like to hunt with the kind of weapon the original American hunters and trappers had to use.

into the barrel through the flash hole, lighting the powder. Flintlocks, on the other hand, like the one I was holding, date back to the early 1600s and have a more complicated firing mechanism.

Suddenly, there he was—a big old whitetail buck sauntered into the clearing and paused to look around for some food.

I took aim. I pulled the trigger, snapping sparks onto the exposed steel frizzen pan. A flash ignited the powder in the pan, sparks shot into the breech to ignite the barrel powder, and a patched bullet launched out of the barrel along with a whoosh of dark smoke.

The bullet flew through the air. The shot just missed the target! The deer vanished back into the woods.

Eight-point buck in dry grass at the National Bison Range, Montana
(RYAN HAGERTY, US FISH & WILDLIFE SERVICE)

I buried my head in my hands and stayed that way for nearly a half hour. I came so close to hitting the deer, but I also came very close to just wounding him, which I never want to do to an animal when hunting. The problem was, it takes so long to reload a muzzle-loader that by the time I got a new shot lined up and I climbed down from the tree, I might never have found the animal if he ran far off while he was wounded.

There were so many steps involved in reloading that it could have taken me well over a half minute. I'd have to pull out the plug from the spout of a powder horn, measure and pour loose powder into the muzzle, shove a patched lead ball into the muzzle with a ramrod, put the ramrod back in its slot, hold up the rifle, open the frizzen, sprinkle some powder onto the pan to prime the charge, snap shut the frizzen, aim, and shoot. By then, the deer could have been well on his way to the next county! If a gust of wind or blast of rain hit the delicate mechanism, or if there was an all-too-frequent misfire, I'd have to start all over again, or give up altogether.

On that day, I gained a whole new appreciation for the courage and skill of early American hunters and pioneers like Daniel Boone. In the face of incredible obstacles and dangers, they helped create a new nation with their bare hands—and long rifles.

Daniel Boone's arrival in Kentucky
(WARD LOCKWOOD, LIBRARY OF CONGRESS)

When European ex-plorers and settlers landed in America in the 1500s and 1600s, they brought two game-changers to the continent: guns and horses. Eventually, horses provided the speed and mobility for both white and Native American hunters to propel themselves across hundreds of miles of territory. At first, the guns they had were pretty useless for hunt-ing. The firing mechanisms of early European shoulder weapons like the matchlock, wheel-lock, snapchance, and harquebus were so complicated and delicate they were prone to misfire, or simply didn't fire at all in rain or wind.

Long rifle hunter, early America
(N. R. Brewer, artist, Library of Congress)

There was one European weapon that held great promise as a hunting rifle in the New World, but only after it was customized for America. It was the short-barreled, large-caliber German-Swiss Jaeger hunting rifle used in the forests of central Europe. In the 1700s, highly skilled gunsmiths in Pennsylvania transformed the Jaeger into what came to be known as the American long rifle, a.k.a. the Pennsylvania or Kentucky rifle. Cut from American maple trees, the new rifle featured long barrels of up to forty-eight inches, with adjustable sights and rifled grooves on the inside of the barrel that gave the bullet a midair twist, all of which improved accuracy.

In a 1924 book, *The Kentucky Rifle*, John Dillin explained how the weapon evolved in the earliest years of the nation:

From a flat bar of soft iron, hand forged into a gun barrel; laboriously bored and rifled with crude tools; fitted with a stock hewn from a maple tree in the neighboring forest; and supplied with a lock hammered to shape on the anvil; an unknown smith, in a shop long since silent, fashioned a rifle which changed the whole course of world history; made possible the settlement of a continent; and ultimately freed our country of foreign domination. Light in weight; graceful in line; economical in consumption of powder and lead; fatally precise; distinctly American; it sprang into immediate popularity; and for a hundred years was a model often slightly varied but never radically changed.

The typical .65 caliber of the European hunting rifles was reduced to an average of .45 for the American long rifle, which was just right for nailing small and medium-sized game in the woods of eastern America.

As a professional hunter and trapper, Daniel Boone was the proud owner of several of these rifles. He depended on them to put food on his growing family's table and to obtain animal skins he could sell for cold, hard cash. According to the great hunter, historian, and president Theodore Roosevelt, many residents of what we now call Appalachia were both hunters and farmers. "Each backwoodsman was not only a small farmer but also a hunter; for his wife and children depended for their meat upon the venison and bear's flesh procured with his rifle. Wild turkeys were plenti-

Bull elk (Gary Zahm, US Fish & Wildlife Service)

ful. Pigeons and squirrels were everywhere. The hunter's standard game was the deer, and after that the bear, the elk was already growing uncommon." Roosevelt added, "He lived out in the woods for many months with no food but meat, and no shelter whatever, unless he made a lean-to of brush or crawled into a hollow syca-more." Hunting was especially crucial for Daniel Boone, as he showed little talent or enthusiasm for farm life.

Tall, lean, and rugged, with muscles like iron, Boone was built perfectly for the frontier. As a Bible-studying, clean-living man of the frontier, he had a simple motto: "To Love and fear God, believe in Jesus Christ, do all the good to my neighbor and myself that I can, and do as little harm as I can help, and trust on God's mercy for the rest."

"Love and fear God, believe in Jesus Christ, do all the good to my neighbor and myself that I can, and do as little harm as I can help, and trust on God's mercy for the rest."
—Daniel Boone

With these ideas in mind, on May 1, 1769, the thirty-four-year-old Boone grabbed his long rifle; slipped into moccasins, buckskin pants, and a fringed hunting shirt; strapped a toma-hawk and knife on his belt; and plopped a beaver-fur hat on his head.

He bade farewell to his wife, Rebecca, and their six children and linked up with his five hunting buddies. Each man carried an American long rifle, a powder horn to pour out gunpowder, and a shot pouch for hand-cast lead balls of .50 to .60 caliber. They loaded gear on their packhorses: cooking and smithing tools, traps, spare rifles, flints, powder, and shot.

They headed west from North Carolina's upper Yadkin River valley and set off on a journey to a largely unknown world, a land called "Kan-Ta-Kee" by Native Americans, where animals were said to teem in incredible abundance.

Daniel Boone was leading the first great deep-penetration journey by white men through the Cumberland Gap into the mostly unknown western territories far from the east coast of North America. Off they went, and they would not return from the wilderness for many months.

Boone was already a hunting and sharpshooting legend, famous for his skills in tracking, decoying, and stalking game—talents he learned from hanging out with Shawnee and Delaware who visited his grandfather's mill when he was a boy. By age eight, he was killing bobwhite quail and rabbits with a wooden throwing stick, and in his early teens, Boone spent days wandering in the woods, sleeping in a log shelter. Soon after he acquired his first long rifle—a short-barreled smooth-bore—he was bagging raccoons and opossums and beating men twice his age in shooting contests, sometimes shooting with only one hand as a handicap, just to show off a bit.

For five weeks, Boone and his comrades pushed westward, and on June 1, 1769, they reached the promised land of Kentucky. Boone climbed a hill called Pilot Knob and beheld a vast landscape of natural beauty, of dense forests and bluegrass meadows, a land that Boone called a "second paradise" and "the Garden of God, unequaled on or earth."

"We found everywhere abundance of wild beasts of all sorts, through this vast forest," Boone later explained. "The buffalo were more frequent than I have seen cattle in the settlements, browsing on the leaves of the cane, or cropping the herbage on those extensive plains, fearless, because ignorant, of the violence of man. Sometimes we saw hundreds in a drove, and the numbers about the salt springs were amazing. In this forest, the habitation of beasts of every kind natural to America, we practiced hunting with great success."

Right away, Boone and his team got down to hunting. They built a little cottage to serve as base camp, with a fire pit and elevated scaffold to protect the meat and hides from predators. Buckskins were most lucrative, so they focused on killing and dressing as many deer as they could find. They used buffalo and bear hides to sleep on and to wrap up the deerskins. Elk skins were fashioned into ropes. In the winter, they switched to trapping for beaver pelts. They went after all kinds of game, like otters, panthers, and turkeys.

On one hunting trip, Boone was by himself—except for his three hounds and two favorite books, the Bible and *Gulliver's Travels*. Sometimes, he sang or talked out loud by a roaring fire. If he sensed Native Americans nearby, he slept in caves or kept a cold camp. He liked to hunt early in the morning when the deer were just up for breakfast and he could stalk them quietly on the dew-moistened ground. To hunt a squirrel in a tree, he aimed not at the squirrel but at the branch beneath it. That way, the fallen squirrel's meat was not damaged. At one point he was taken prisoner by Shawnee, who considered him a poacher on their land (and let's face it, he sort of was) and confiscated a year's worth of his skins and pelts, but he was released with a warning: if you come here again, "you may be sure the wasps and yellow-jackets will sting you severely."

Daniel Boone was released with a warning: if you come here again, "you may be sure the wasps and yellow-jackets will sting you severely."

Before the hunters returned to their families at the end of 1770, Boone described a scene of spiritual revelation:

I had gained the summit of a commanding ridge, and, looking round with astonishing delight, beheld the ample plains, the beauteous tracts below. On the other hand, I surveyed the famous river Ohio, that rolled in silent dignity, marking the western boundary of Kentucky with inconceivable grandeur. At a vast distance I beheld the mountains lift their venerable brows, and penetrate the clouds. All things were still. I kindled a fire near a fountain of sweet water, and feasted on the loin of a buck, which a few hours before

I had killed. The sullen shades of night soon overspread the whole hemisphere, and the earth seemed to gasp after the hovering moisture.

In 1773 Boone went back to Kentucky, hoping to launch a permanent settlement but was devastated when a band of Cherokees captured, tortured, and killed his sixteen-year-old son, James. Boone kept trying, however, and returned again in 1775 to open up the route that became known as Boone's Trace, or the Wilderness Road, and start Fortress Boonesborough, a new settlement on the Kentucky River that eventually became a major gateway for westbound settlers.

In 1778, Boone and twenty-nine men were seized by a force of pro-British Native American warriors and taken to Detroit as prisoners. The Native Americans were so impressed by Boone that they performed a ceremony to adopt him into their tribe, complete with a ritual dunking in the river to clean the white blood out of him, head shaving, feathers, ribbons, and face painting. Having little choice in the matter, Boone played along as a tribal member for several months, until he overheard that the Native Americans planned to attack Boonesborough. He slipped off to issue a warning. He recalled, "On the 16th of June, before sunrise, I departed in the most secret manner, and arrived at Boonesborough on the 20th after a journey of 160 miles, during which I had but one meal." Boone and his fellow settlers managed to repulse the attack.

American hunters, nineteenth century (F. O. C. DARLEY, LIBRARY OF CONGRESS)

Daniel Boone went on long hunts for more than sixty years, from age fifteen to eighty-three. Looking back on his life in the rough wilderness of early America, Boone recalled, "My footsteps have often been marked with blood," and his adventures took a heavy toll. "Two darling sons and a brother have I lost by savage [Native American] hands, which have also taken from me forty valuable horses, and an abundance of cattle. Many dark and sleepless nights have I been a companion for owls, separated from the cheerful society of men, scorched by the summer's sun, and pinched by the winter's cold—an instrument ordained to settle the wilderness."

Boone may have known his share of bloodshed and sadness, but he left a great mark on history.

Armed with his hunting rifle and Bible, Daniel Boone helped push the borders of the American colonies westward by many thousands of square miles. Personally, he traveled an incredibly wide area on foot, on horseback, and by boat—from eastern Pennsylvania down to Florida, through Maryland, Virginia, Tennessee, North Carolina, and Kentucky into what is now Michigan and Ohio, across the Mississippi and up the Missouri River.

In the process, he laid the territorial foundations for much of what would come to be known as the United States. He helped kick off the United States' westward migration and the eventual power shift from Native Americans to European settlers.

Thanks to Daniel Boone, a new national American identity was created—born from the likes of another great American hunter, a strapping fellow from Virginia by the name of George Washington.

It is the American heritage to carry a gun
afield as did our forefathers
and to take fish from the lakes and streams.
They killed game and caught fish to sustain life;
we hunt and fish for health and happiness.

—Dan Holland, *Good Shot: A Book of Rod, Gun, and Camera*

CHAPTER 4

THE FOUNDING HUNTERS

The father of America was a hard-core hunting buff.

Back in the 1700s, foxhunting was all the rage in rural Virginia among members of the English colonial gentry like George Washington, a man who became widely known as one of the finest equestrians, and most enthusiastic foxhunters, in America. His good friend Thomas Jefferson said that Washington was "the best horseman of his age, and the most graceful figure that could be seen on horseback."

As often as he could, starting in his late twenties and into the American Revolution, Washington would saddle up on one of his fine horses at his Mount Vernon estate, summon his pack of dogs, meet up with friends, and go "riding to hounds." Then, led by the dogs' noses, the group would charge after a fox, sometimes for hours and many miles through the countryside, across hills and fences. At the end of a chase, the fox would be run up into a tree, caught, or killed.

This was hunting purely for sport, not for food, as you just can't eat a fox. It tastes flat-out terrible, or so I'm told. In fact, a critic once called foxhunting "the inexcusable chasing the inedible." But George Washington loved foxhunting as much as I love hunting duck and deer, in his case probably because it gave him endless hours of outdoor exercise on horseback. He loved his hounds, too, and gave them colorful names like Mopsey, Pilot, Tartar, Jupiter, Trueman, Tipler, Truelove, Juno, Dutchess, Ragman, Countess, Lady, Searcher, Rover, Vulcan, Singer, Music, and, naturally, Sweetlips. Sometimes, George took his wife, Martha, along on a foxhunt. She rode her own horse and wore a big red shawl for maximum visibility.

Founding hunter George Washington returns from a foxhunt at Mount Vernon (LIBRARY OF CONGRESS)

When you read Washington's diary, it seems like he spent nearly all his spare time foxhunting from 1759 to 1774. Here are just a few excerpts, which I've simplified a bit from the original eighteenth-century spelling and grammar:

> Went fox hunting with the gentlemen who came here yesterday. After a very early breakfast, found a fox just back of Muddy Hole Plantation and after a chase of an hour and a quarter with my dogs we put him into a hollow tree, in which we fastened him, and put up another fox which, in an hour and thirteen minutes was killed.

> After an early breakfast George Washington [Washington's nephew, also of the same name], Mr. Shaw and Myself went into the woods back of Muddy Hole Plantation a hunting and were joined by Mr. Lund Washington and Mr. William Peake. We found a fox near Colonel Mason's Plantation on Little Hunting Creek. In about fifty Minutes [the fox was] killed up in an open field of Colonel Mason's, every rider and every dog being present at the Death.

I've always admired Washington, but the day I really started loving him most was when I discovered he was a duck man through and through. That's right: the father of our nation was a devoted shooter and duck hunter. "Went a ducking between breakfast and dinner and killed two mallards and five bald faces," Washington once wrote in his diary. Another time, he noted, "I went to the Creek but not across it. Killed two ducks, namely a sprig tail and a teal."

George Washington shared something in common with us in the Robertson family—his property was overflowing with ducks. A visitor to Mount Vernon in 1785 wrote of Washington's land, "The situation is a heavenly one, upon one of the finest rivers in the world [the Chesapeake]. I suppose I saw thousands of wild ducks upon it, all within gunshot."

But just like the Robertson family, the general was strict about his property, and his ducks.

Like the Robertson family, General Washington was strict about his property, and his ducks.

In 1787 a man asked permission to shoot at Mount Vernon. Washington told him to forget it, period. He decided, "No person whatever shall hunt upon my grounds or waters," because he figured if he let one person shoot, he'd have to let everyone else too, or they'd be offended. He wrote, "My strict and positive orders to all my people are if they hear a gun fired upon my land to go immediately in pursuit of it." He continued, "Besides, as I have not lost my relish for this sport when I find time to indulge myself in it, and gentlemen who come to the House are pleased with it, it is my wish not to have game within my jurisdiction disturbed." In other words, he wanted the birds just for his own table.

When Washington became president, he got too busy to do much hunting, and a bad fall from a horse in 1787 that messed up his back spelled an end to his days of "riding to hounds."

But this greatest of men never lost his taste for duck.

One day, late in his life and after he'd retired from the presidency, George Washington met some friends for dinner at Gadsby's Tavern at the City Hotel in Alexandria.

The proprietor, a renowned host named John Gadsby, came over to take Washington's order and mentioned that he had a supply of fine canvas-back ducks in the larder.

"Very good, sir," said Washington as a smile spread across his face, "give us some of them, with a chafing-dish, some hominy, and a bottle of good Madeira, and we shall not complain."

———

THOMAS JEFFERSON was another Virginia boy and founding father with deep family roots in hunting.

According to Jefferson family history, Jefferson's introduction to hunting started rather unceremoniously when Jefferson was ten years old. His father gave him a rifle and sent him into the woods by himself to shoot some dinner.

When Jefferson was ten years old, his father gave him a rifle and sent him into the woods by himself to shoot some dinner.

Young Jefferson wandered around without seeing any game. Then, spotting a wild turkey in a pen, he had an idea. He grabbed the bird, tied it to a tree, shot it, and toted it back home triumphantly.

By age fourteen, Jefferson was more properly hunting deer, turkeys, and foxes in the mountains, and he soon became an ardent foxhunter as well. One biographer, James Parton, wrote in 1877 that "[Jefferson] was a keen hunter, as eager after a fox as Washington himself, swift of foot and sound of wind, coming in fresh and alert after a long day's clambering hunt."

In 1785, Jefferson wrote to his fifteen-year-old nephew Peter Carr about what he recommended as the best form of exercise: "I advise the gun. While this gives a moderate exercise to the body, it gives boldness, enterprise, and independence to the mind. Games played with the ball, and others of that nature, are too violent for the body, and stamp no character on the mind. Let your gun, therefore, be the constant companion of your walks."

Isaac Jefferson, one of the slaves at Jefferson's estate Monticello, recalled that Jefferson shot "squirrels and partridges; kept five or six guns." He noted that unlike his ten-year-old self, Jefferson would never shoot a still animal, because he didn't want to take advantage of it; Jefferson would always "scare him up first."

Like George Washington, Thomas Jefferson sometimes had a problem with poachers on his land. But he had a get-tough policy that was stricter than Washington's.

Whenever he heard that outside hunters were trespassing on his deer park at Monticello, the six-foot-three-inch Jefferson would grab his gun, march down to confront the hunters face-to-face, and order them to scram. They always did.

ONE OF THE GREATEST ADVENTURES in American history began in 1804, when President Jefferson sent thirty-three men on a journey of exploration across the young nation.

You could also say it was it one of the most historic hunting trips ever made.

Jefferson called it the Corps of Discovery Expedition, and it became known as the Lewis and Clark Expedition, after its leaders, the ex-army volunteers Captain Meriwether Lewis and Second Lieutenant William Clark. It would take them over two years to make the voyage, and they had to live off the land as subsistence

American hunting scene (CURRIER & IVES, CIRCA 1863, LIBRARY OF CONGRESS)

hunters along the way. It required an average of four deer, an elk, or one buffalo to supply the expedition for a single twenty-four-hour period.

Their mission was to stage a round-trip journey from Saint Louis to the Pacific Coast and back—on foot, horseback, and boat—to find and map a transcontinental water route to the Pacific through the vast territory recently bought from France that became known as the Louisiana Purchase. Along the way, they would record observations on geography, plants, animals, climate, and the customs of Native American residents.

One of the superstars of the Lewis and Clark adventure was the expedition's chief hunter, a Shawnee-born man named George Drouillard. Under his supervision, expedition members killed no fewer than 1,750 big-game animals, which they used primarily for food, including about 1,000 deer, 375 elks, 230 buffaloes, 60 antelopes, 35 bighorn sheep, 23 black bears, and 43 grizzly bears. The expedition gave the non–Native American world its first detailed information on a wide variety of creatures, like the mule deer, coyote, white-tailed jackrabbit, bighorn sheep, magpie, and many more.

Traveling across the plains, Captain Lewis noted in his journal, "Game is still very abundant. We can hardly cast our eye in any direction without perceiving deer, Elk, Buffalo or Antelopes. The quantity of wolves appear to increase in the same proportion." On May 5, 1805, he wrote,

A fine morning. I walked on shore until 8 AM when we halted for breakfast and in the course of my walk killed a deer which I carried about a mile and a half to the river, it was in good order. . . . As usual saw a great quantity of game today; Buffaloe Elk and goats or Antelopes feeding in every direction; we kill whatever we wish, the buffaloe furnish us with fine veal and fat beef, we also have venison and beaver tales when we wish them; the flesh of the Elk and goat are less esteemed, and certainly are inferior. We have not been able to take any fish for some time past. The country is as yesterday beautiful in the extreme.

Lewis and Clark brought along an impressive arsenal of weapons and gear for hunting and self-defense, nearly two tons' worth. According to their supply report, they carried:

1 Pair Pocket Pistols, 1 Pair Horseman's Pistols, 15 Rifles [many were probably Harpers Ferry Model 1792s, a heavier, military-grade version of the Kentucky rifle], 15 Powder Horns and Pouches, 15 pairs of bullet molds, 15 wipers or gun worms, 15 ball screws, Extra Parts of Locks and Tools for Repairing Arms, 15 Gun Slings, 500 Rifle Flints, 420 Pounds of Sheet Lead for Bullets, 176 Pounds of Gunpowder, 52 Leaden Canisters for Gunpowder, and 1 Long-Barreled Air Rifle.

Hunting elk in the Black Hills (ALFRED JACOB MILLER, WALTERS ART MUSEUM)

On top of this, their hired French boatmen toted personal weapons like trade rifles, Kentucky long rifles, and English "Fusils," or shotguns. A small swivel cannon was fastened to the bow of their keelboat, and a "blunderbuss," or large-bore shotgun, was mounted on the stern.

But by far the most amazing hunting gun carried on the Lewis and Clark Expedition was an extremely high-tech, prototype weapon called the Girandoni air rifle. In an age of single-shot, slow-loading muzzle-loaders, the Girandoni was an unheard-of twenty-two-shot *repeating* rifle, with a detachable reservoir on the gun butt that held .462-caliber lead bullets. It seemed like the Lamborghini of rifles.

In theory, the Austrian-designed Girandoni was the perfect weapon for Lewis and Clark. It was powered by compressed air, not gunpowder, and completely noiseless, so it didn't alert animals or hostile natives to their presence. There was no smoke and powder to gum up the lock and barrel. The reloading action was simple: a metal tube on the side of the barrel held up to twenty-two bullets that could be loaded in one at a time to the firing chamber simply by pushing a plunger sideways. In the hands of a skilled operator, it could place ten shots into a pattern the size of a quarter from fifty feet away, and it had the power to knock down a medium-sized deer. It greatly impressed the many local Native Americans they met along the way, as Captain Clark wrote of a meeting on October 29, 1804, "After the council was over, we shot the air gun, which appeared to astonish the natives much."

In practice, though, the Girandoni air rifle had some fatal flaws. It was fragile and delicate. If you dropped it or knocked it hard, it was nearly unfixable. But the main problem was the mechanics of pressurizing the air. To fill a twenty-two-shot bullet reservoir, or clip, you needed to crank a hand pump over a thousand times. In the time it took to reload a new clip, you might be sprawled out exhausted on the prairie or become an after-dinner snack for a grizzly bear. This is why you almost never hear of Girandoni rifles anymore.

> In the time it took to reload a new clip in the Girandoni, you might be sprawled out exhausted on the prairie or become an after-dinner snack for a grizzly bear.

Speaking of grizzly bears, they proved to be by far the most dangerous animals encountered by Lewis and Clark on their excellent adventure. They were confronted by grizzlies no fewer than forty times during the mission. Tens of thousands of these fearless, enormous animals ranged across the Rocky Mountains, and at first they seemed like flesh-and-blood monsters to the explorers. A mature male could weigh up to nine hundred pounds and raise up on its haunches to a height of eight feet, and gallop as much as four miles at a speed of thirty miles an hour. On May 5, 1805, Clark wrote, "In the evening we saw a Brown or Grisley beare on a sand beech, I went out with one man Geo Drewyer [Drouillard] & Killed the bear, which was verry large and a turrible looking animal, which we found verry hard to kill we Shot ten Balls into him before we killed him."

Nine days later, on May 14, 1805, Lewis wrote of another hair-raising encounter with a grizzly:

Capt. Clark and Drewyer killed the largest brown [grizzly] bear this evening which we have yet seen. It was a most tremendous looking animal, and extremely hard to kill. Notwithstanding he had five balls through his lungs and five others in various parts he swam more than half the distance across the river to a sandbar and it was at least twenty minutes before he died. He did not attempt to attack, but fled and made the most tremendous roaring from the moment he was shot. We had no means of weighing this monster; Capt. Clark thought he would weigh 500 lbs. For my own part I think the estimate too small by 100 lbs. He measured 8 Feet 7½ Inches from the nose to the extremety of the hind feet, 5 F. 10½ inch arround the breast.

Captain Lewis hunts bear on the epic Lewis and Clark journey (LIBRARY OF CONGRESS)

Nourished and sustained by their by constant hunting of big and small game, Lewis and Clark reached the Pacific Ocean, safely made it back to Saint Louis, and gave President Thomas Jefferson a full report on their epic voyage.

Along the way they pioneered water routes to the Pacific, encountered fifty Native American tribes, discovered three hundred species of animals and plants not known to science, established a firm claim on vast new American territories, and symbolically linked the young nation to its western destiny.

It was the greatest hunt in American history.

The way of the hunter is, then, the way finally of passion,
a passion that is every bit as old as those hills
it carries us through and into our home in the game fields
filled with real life.
—Thomas McIntyre, *The Way of the Hunter*

CHAPTER 5

THE AGE OF THE MOUNTAIN MEN

Lewis and Clark's expedition kicked off a booming fur trade in the West, and a new breed of character flooded into the new territories to explore, hunt, and especially trap for lucrative beaver skins.

They were called the mountain men, and their time in the North American Rocky Mountains spanned from 1810 to the 1880s, with its peak in the 1840s. And during their heyday, there was a trapper who was one of the toughest mountain men of all. His name was John Colter. He was a shy, blue-eyed, Virginia-born hunter and tracker who fell in love with the Northwest while serving as a soldier in Lewis and Clark's Corps of Discovery, and he yearned to continue exploring and make a killing in the trapping business.

On Lewis and Clark's expedition, he had a rough start—one time he was busted for sneaking off to a whiskey store at Camp Wood, upriver from Saint Louis, and getting drunk on New Year's Eve. Another time he threatened to shoot an officer. He begged forgiveness and promised to do better. Lewis and Clark gave him a second chance, and Colter knuckled down and became one of the best scouts and boatmen on the mission. Lewis and Clark gave him permission to stay behind and try his luck at beaver trapping on the Upper Missouri.

In the fall of 1807 John Colter strapped on a hunting rifle and a thirty-pound pack filled with jerky, gunpowder, lead, a blanket, and gifts for the Native Americans and set off west on a legendary voyage that became known as "Colter's Walk." Over the next few months he walked over some of the highest mountains in Wyoming; became the first white man to see the staggering beauty of the Teton Range, Jackson Hole, and Yellowstone Valley; and returned in the spring of 1808 with tales of vast lakes and smoking geysers. In that one winter journey, he managed to cover a stunning five hundred miles, alone, on foot.

Colter's most hair-raising adventure occurred later in 1808, when he and his buddy John Potts set off west up the Yellowstone River toward the Three Forks of the Missouri, where the beavers were plentiful. The two men set traps all along the rivers, until one day they were suddenly confronted by a large force of several hundred Blackfoot who appeared on both banks of the river.

Colter was working on a trap when the Native Americans

shouted for the white men to come over. He inconspicuously slipped his trap back in the water and waded ashore. Potts, in the boat, refused to comply. Shots and arrows were exchanged, and Potts and a Native American were killed. Potts's body was riddled with arrows. The deceased Native American's enraged relatives demanded a summary field execution of Colter, but a senior Native American warrior had an idea to combine justice with a little outdoor fun.

Pueblo hunter (LIBRARY OF CONGRESS)

"Can you run fast?" he asked Colter, who was familiar with the Blackfoot language.

Colter lied, saying he was a terribly slow runner. In fact, he was a powerful all-around mountain athlete. But sensing what was coming next, he figured that with odds like this, he'd need all the head start he could get.

Colter was stripped buck naked and sent several hundred yards ahead on the field. Then the Native Americans charged him, spears and axes in their hands. They hadn't reckoned on his speed; Colter was an incredibly fast and strong runner, and he stayed ahead of his pursuers, though his feet were seriously banged up by the rough ground. Blood gushed from his nose, probably from overexertion in the thin mountain air.

After several miles, only one Native American could keep up with him. The naked Colter suddenly turned and lunged for the Native American's spear. The fast-running Native American was so surprised that he tripped and somersaulted as he attempted to chuck a spear into Colter. Colter killed him, took the warrior's spear and blanket, and scurried farther down the river, where he hid under driftwood with only his nose above the water. For hours, the Native Americans searched for him, at one point walking directly over the logs Colter was hiding under, but they eventually gave up the hunt.

Barefoot and stark naked except for the blanket, John Colter somehow managed to walk more than two hundred miles through the wilderness, in chilly autumn weather, to safety—living on berries and apples along the way. He was sunburned and covered in cuts and blisters, but he was alive.

Incredibly, the next year, Colter decided to go back to the exact same spot where he was nearly killed so he could pick up the beaver trap he'd left in the river. On the way, he was again nearly killed by Blackfoot warriors, so he did the sensible thing: he turned tail and settled down in safer country back east, where he married and had a son. Colter's Run made him a legend among his fellow mountain men.

———

Speaking of American mountain men, let me tell you about one of the greatest of all. His name was Jedediah Smith.

He was a Bible-studying, prayer-loving, pious Methodist from upstate New York who was born in 1799, the year George Washington died, and became a legendary hunter, trapper, fur trader, cartographer, and explorer. He wound up exploring more of America than any other American of his time. He never smoked, never drank, and rarely even told a joke. Instead, he was consumed with a burning vision to travel far into the unknown lands of the American West. "I wanted to be the first to view a country on which the eyes of a white man had never gazed," he explained, "and to follow the course of rivers that run through a new land."

At twenty-two years of age, he stuffed a copy of Lewis and Clark's travel journals in his pack and signed up with General William Ashley's beaver-trapping expedition to the Upper Missouri. He quickly mastered all the skills of a hunter and mountain man, including hunting buffaloes and all kinds of wild game.

And let me tell you, this boy was tough! One day, along the Cheyenne River, Smith was stalked and tackled by a king-sized grizzly bear. A mortal wrestling match ensued, and it was a beat-down worthy of a horror movie on late-night cable TV.

The beast ripped Smith's sides clean open with his claws. He smashed his ribs. Then he stuffed Smith's head inside his mouth like a big piece of raw steak and chomped down his powerful jaws for a burst of flavor. The grizzly took a hearty chew on poor Smith, separating a good-size chunk of his scalp and ear from his head.

The grizzly took a hearty chew on poor Smith, separating a good-size chunk of his scalp and ear from his head.

For unknown reasons, which may or may not have been related to taste, the bear suddenly stopped eating, released Smith, and backed off, giving Smith's companions just enough time to evacuate him to safety. Smith's scalp was hanging off his head. In an impressive feat of backwoods battlefield surgery, Smith's buddy Jim Clyman sewed his head back together. Clyman tried his best with the scalp but figured the ear was a total goner. Smith insisted that he give it a shot. Clyman recalled, "I put my needle sticking it through and through and over and over laying the lacerated parts together as nice as I could with my hands." To their surprise, Clyman fixed Smith up well enough to finish their journey. From then on, Smith wore long hair to conceal the damage.

At one point, when Smith and his party were surrounded on the banks of the Colorado River by hundreds of Mojave bent on wiping them out, they pulled some trees together to make a make-shift mini-fort with breastworks.

They made lances out of butcher knives lashed on top of poles and braced themselves for a final stand. When the Mojaves came close enough, Smith ordered his men to open fire, and they caused enough pain for the Native Americans to finally scatter. It was a super-close shave, but Smith and his crew made it all the way to the San Bernardino Valley in California, which is about as close to paradise as you can get on this earth. Outside of the woods of Northeast Louisiana, that is.

In 1824, Smith achieved his greatest glory in a feat that directly shaped American history. He led a group of Ashley's men on a deep-penetration voyage far into the Central Rockies, and in the process, he discovered the great South Pass through the moun-tains, opening up a major path for America to expand to Califor-nia and the Pacific. Until then, white hunters and trappers knew of no way through the Rockies other than the hazardous Missouri River route pioneered by Lewis and Clark. Jedediah Smith made friends with some Crow and learned of the easy pass through the mountains, which is in present-day Wyoming.

In fact, Smith's discovery of South Pass was more like a "redis-covery," as employees of John Jacob Astor's Pacific Fur Company had gone through it twelve years earlier on the way from the Pacific to Saint Louis. Even though their travel journal was given to President James Madison and published in France, nobody con-nected the dots. The South Pass was not publicized, and the discovery fell through the cracks until Jedediah Smith came along.

Hunting buffaloes in the US (GEORGE CATLIN, 1844, LIBRARY AND ARCHIVES CANADA)

The South Pass was a broad, gentle prairie "super-highway" that was perfect for wagon traffic, and it united the Pacific and Atlantic watersheds at the Continental Divide. Between 1848 and the opening of the transcontinental railroads in 1868–69, the South Pass handled some five hundred thousand travelers searching for a new life in the West.

On top of his epic discovery of the South Pass, before he turned thirty, Smith explored the Colorado lowlands and the Great Salt Lake, and he led the first expeditions that took a white man through the Central Rockies and American Southwest via the Salt Lake frontier, the Colorado River, and the Mojave Desert, clear over to California. He became the first white explorer to cross the Sierra Nevada and the Great Basin and to reach the Oregon Country over land by journeying north along the coast of California.

His trips provided the foundation of new, accurate maps of the Pacific West—including one map produced in 1830–31 that was called "a landmark in mapping of the American West." Not bad for a boy from New York, wouldn't you say?

He was rightly proud of his accomplishments, writing in his journal, "I started into the mountains, with the determination of becoming a first-rate hunter, of making myself thoroughly acquainted with the character and habits of the Native Americans, of tracing out the sources of the Columbia River and following it to its mouth; and of making the whole profitable to me, and I have perfectly succeeded."

In 1830, he cashed out his shares in the highly profitable Rocky Mountain Fur Company in hopes of settling down and starting a responsible family life on a nice little estate he bought in Saint Louis. But he agreed to go on one last expedition for the new owners, and that's what did him in.

In 1831, while leading a trading caravan on the Santa Fe Trail near the Cimarron River, he set off in search of water and was killed in a shoot-out and lance attack by mounted Comanche. He was thirty-two years old. They never found his body, so he remains out there somewhere under the open sky. He's mostly forgotten now; few people today remember his name or the incredible things he did, unless you're in California and you visit Jedediah Smith Redwoods State Park, the Jedediah Smith Memorial Trail, or the Smith River, and you stop to look up who they're named after.

I've known more than a few mountain men in my life, and

plenty more folks who've claimed to be one. But few can touch the glory achieved by Jedediah Smith.

ANOTHER LEGENDARY early American hunter was Davy Crockett, the "King of the Wild Frontier." The Tennessee-born Crockett grew up on the Tennessee frontier as a skilled hunter and rifleman who reportedly described himself as "half horse and half alligator, a little touched with the snapping turtle; [I] can wade the Mississippi, leap the Ohio, ride upon a streak of lightning, slide down a honey locust and not get scratched, [and] whip my weight in wild cats."

Davy Crockett described himself as "half horse and half alligator, a little touched with the snapping turtle."

He developed into an expert marksman as a teenager and regularly won shooting contests. He was also an incredibly successful bear hunter who reportedly killed 105 bears in less than one year. He nicknamed his long rifle "Old Betsy." In 1815, he signed up for Andrew Jackson's intensely bloody expedition against the Creek but was horrified at the slaughter, including one episode when he witnessed a native village surrounded and the residents "shot like dogs." Crockett's fame as a hunter and backwoods philosopher earned him national celebrity and eight years in Congress, and he died at the Alamo at age fifty, hunting rifle in his hand.

The life of professional trappers and hunters in the early days of America was a rugged, primitive existence in which man fully entered nature and became a part of it. "The hunter is the arch-type of freedom," wrote the great hunter Theodore Roosevelt.

His well-being rests in no man's hands save his own. He chops down and hews out the logs for his hut, or perhaps makes merely a rude dug-out in the side of a hill, with a skin roof, and skin flaps for the door. He buys a little flour and salt, and in times of plenty also sugar and tea; but not much, for it must all be carried hundreds of miles on the backs of his shaggy pack-ponies. In one corner of the hut, a bunk covered with deer-skins forms his bed; a kettle and a frying-pan may be all his cooking-utensils. When he can get no fresh meat he falls back on his stock of jerked veni-son, dried in long strips over the fire or in the sun.

The big money for American beaver fur trappers and moun-tain men was largely gone with the collapse of the fur trade in the early 1840s, due largely to fickle tastes in fashion in the export market to Europe. For a while, imported fur hats were all the rage in London and Paris, then one day they were "out," and so was much of the trappers' business.

But the mountain men, and the fur companies that many of

them worked for, explored vast new territories of America and helped build out the wilderness paths and emigrant trails that eventually were widened into wagon roads that carried thousands of Americans westward.

Like many other hunters and frontiersmen and women, they helped lay the foundation for America.

Next time you travel out to California, take a moment to think about Jedediah Smith and the adventures he opened up for all of us. He's one of the men who opened up the golden door for Americans to achieve our western destiny. And while you're at it, why don't you take a moment to thank him and thank God for all the mountain men and women who helped create our nation?

A wild-bear chace, didst never see?
Then hast thou lived in vain.

—Abraham Lincoln, "The Bear Hunt"

CHAPTER 6

THE HUNDRED-YEAR WAR AGAINST THE GRIZZLIES

As soon as non–Native American hunters and trappers began penetrating the Rocky Mountains, they came face-to-face with a truly terrifying enemy—the grizzly bear.

For the next century, a bloody, brutal, long-forgotten war raged across the mountains.

It was the Hundred-Year War Against the Grizzlies, and it was an epic historical contest between man and beast that resulted in scores of human casualties and thousands of grizzlies killed. It was a savage, bloody war for territory, and the bears held the upper hand and home-field advantage.

At first, the grizzlies ruled most of the mountainous West and man was powerless to challenge them. When European settlers arrived, there were some one hundred thousand bears in the West, from Alaska clear down to Mexico. They were enormous, power-ful, and adaptable creatures and had no natural predators. They could run fast, up to thirty-five miles an hour in a short sprint, and they were fine swimmers as well. In addition to plants, they mauled, killed, and ate most anything that moved—fish, ground squirrels, cows, deer, moose, steers, and sheep, you name it. They thrived not only in the mountains but in the prairies, woodlands, forests, and meadows, and along rivers and streams.

Fed-up settlers tried everything to kill the grizzly, from poison and traps to group-hunting posses and burning and clearing the land, but there were always too many bears and not enough peo-ple. One crafty grizzly was cred-ited with killing a thousand sheep in fifteen years, and he was never caught. Every few days he would snatch a sheep and vanish back into the woods.

If all you had was the smoothbore trade rifle, you could put twenty or thirty rounds in the bear and all that would happen was you'd annoy him before he started snacking on you.

From the hunter's point of view, the main problem was fire-power. If you came upon a griz-zly and all you had was a low-muzzle-velocity, flintlock American long rifle firing .45 or .50 caliber, you hardly had a prayer, unless you got off a very lucky head or heart shot. The griz-zly would make short work of you before you could reload, which probably wouldn't have much mattered anyway, because you were a goner. And if all you had was the smoothbore trade rifle, you could put twenty or thirty rounds in the bear and all that would happen was you'd annoy him before he started snacking on you.

Imagine you're one of the first American hunters carefully tip-toeing along an old Native American forest trail in what is now Colorado. It's virgin territory, and you may be the first non–Native American to lay eyes on the breathtaking beauty of this part of the Rockies, the pine forests and peaceful meadows that sweep up to heavenly, snow-capped peaks.

You're walking through the woods, and you've got your trusty small-bore flintlock American long rifle in your hands, locked and loaded; your gear strapped around your shoulder; a King James Bible in your pack; and a wide-brimmed hat plopped on your head.

Suddenly there's a rustle somewhere in the sloping woods above you, and a demonic growl so unearthly it might have come from hell itself.

You glance up and absorb the sight of an eight-foot-tall monster thirty yards away, charging downhill at you with incredible speed. You swing your rifle up and squeeze off a round at the creature's brain. It's a perfect head shot. Only trouble is, your little bullet bounces off the granitelike head of your target, who acts like he didn't feel a thing. The game's over in less than ten seconds and so are you.

This kind of scenario is exactly what happened to a mountain man named Hugh Glass one day in August 1823, only he didn't have time to fire a shot before the grizzly attacked him.

Early American grizzly bear hunt (LIBRARY OF CONGRESS)

Glass was over forty years old, practically elderly by the standards of the time, and he had answered a "help wanted" ad in the *Missouri Gazette and Public Adviser* placed by General William Ashley, which announced that a team of one hundred men would be selected for a fur-trading mission up the Missouri River.

While scouting near the forks of the Grand River in present-day Perkins County, South Dakota, Glass stumbled into a thicket and startled a mama grizzly bear and her two cubs. Very bad, right? The bear charged, picked up Glass, and pounded him onto the ground, knocking Glass's rifle away from him in the process. After swiping a hunk of flesh off of Glass and tossing it to her children, the bear chased Glass up a tree and then pulled him down. Hand-to-paw combat ensued, with Glass frantically stabbing the beast with his knife as the bear kept on mauling him.

Hearing Glass's screams, two of his partners, Jim Bridger and John Fitzgerald, ran over to help, poured enough bullets into the bear to kill her, and rolled her off of poor Glass, who was a horribly injured, bloody mess. They dragged Glass back to their camp, where expedition boss Andrew Henry had a long look at Glass and said he was as good as dead, probably in a few hours, tops. Bridger and Fitzgerald volunteered to stay with what remained of Glass, bandage him up as best they could, decently bury him when he died, and then catch up with the group.

They sat and waited. And waited. They dug a shallow grave for Glass, who was unconscious. But he wouldn't die. After three days, Fitzgerald, afraid of hostile Native Americans in the region, talked Bridger into taking all of Glass's belongings, including his food, weapons, and ammo, and taking off. They rejoined their expedition and reported that Glass was dead, which seemed very close to the truth.

But in fact, Glass was alive. He woke up one day about a week after the attack to find himself all alone, lying in a shallow grave and covered by a bearskin hide, some leaves, and dirt.

His leg was broken, his back was gashed open from his ribs to his backside, his scalp was nearly torn off, he had lost lots of blood, and his wounds were festering. He was two hundred miles from the nearest American outpost, at Fort Kiowa on the Missouri. On September 9, 1823, he set off.

Glass set his own leg, wrapped himself in the bearskin hide, and began crawling around. To forestall gangrene, Glass laid his wounded back on a decaying log to enable maggots to devour and clean his rotting flesh.

To forestall gangrene, Glass laid his wounded back on a decaying log to enable maggots to devour and clean his rotting flesh.

When he spotted a rattlesnake moving slowly and lazily because it was enjoying a bird gorging its belly, he smashed it with a rock. It was tasty. Later, he came across two wolves who were chowing down on a buffalo calf. Glass shooed off the wolves, who were probably horrified by the sight of the maimed mountain man, and helped himself to chunks of raw buffalo flesh. For several days he feasted on the carcass, savoring the nutritious liver, heart, and intestines.

Over the next weeks, Hugh Glass crawled, tumbled, and staggered toward salvation, dodging Native Americans and stampeding buffaloes, nourished by bugs, wild berries and roots, snakes, and dead animals that he found on the ground. He passed out numerous times from infection and fever. According to one account, he woke up one time to find a grizzly bear licking his wounds. At another point he was aided by friendly Native Americans who fed him, helped stitch him up a bit, and gave him a few weapons. He made it to the Cheyenne River, built a raft from a dead tree, and floated himself toward Fort Kiowa on the Missouri River, which he finally reached six weeks after the original attack. He had crossed over two hundred miles.

All along the way, Hugh Glass was propelled by one idea: to track down and kill Jim Bridger and John Fitzgerald, the two men who had abandoned him in his grave. Once he had recovered from a months-long recuperation, Glass set off for revenge.

He found the young Jim Bridger at a fur-trading station on the Yellowstone River near the mouth of the Bighorn River. The stunned nineteen-year-old stared at the apparition of a man he thought for sure was dead.

"It's Glass, Bridger—the one you left to die, and not only left, but robbed," growled Glass. "Robbed of them things as might have helped him survive, alone and crippled, on the plains. I came back because I swore I'd put you under. I had that notion in front of me when I crawled across the prairie starving and walked up the river alone, just to get this one job done!"

Glass had murder on his mind, but he hesitated. The terrified kid looked so young. Glass changed his mind. "But I see you're ashamed and sorry," he said. "I think you might have stayed by me if Fitzgerald hadn't got on you. You don't have to be afraid of me. I forgive you. You're just a kid." An exhausted Glass sat down, someone passed him a glass of whiskey, and he passed out cold.

It took Hugh Glass nearly a year after the attack to track down

John Fitzgerald all the way to Fort Atkinson, Wisconsin, where he was serving in the United States Army. Glass blustered his way into the office of Fitzgerald's commanding officer, Captain Riley, demanding justice. Fitzgerald was brought in.

Bull elk in a Montana meadow (Ryan Hagerty, US Fish & Wildlife Service)

"You ran out on me dyin!" raged Glass, who by now had probably rehearsed the speech a thousand times in his brain. "You was paid well enough, and you said you'd stay until I was good or gone down. But you got scared and run off. And you stole what I might have lived by. Stole it so you could get some money that wasn't yours and so nobody'd know what you done. Well, I count you got something to think on the rest of your string!" Glass demanded that he be allowed to shoot Fitzgerald, who still had the rifle he'd swiped from Glass when he left him for dead, but the captain declined. The captain offered to take up a collection from sympathetic soldiers to outfit Glass with some gear and send him on his way, and Glass cooled down and accepted, grabbing his gun back on the way out.

Glass lived another decade as a fur trader and professional hunter and then returned to the magnificent promised lands of the Upper Missouri. When he was scalped and killed in an Native American attack in 1833, he was still toting the same rifle that the mama grizzly bear had knocked out of his hands in South Dakota. You could say that none of this would have happened if Glass were toting a truly good rifle on that day, like a fast-shooting, fast-reloading gun with the power to knock down a grizzly bear.

Trouble was, no such gun existed. Yet.

———

BUT THEN, in the mid-nineteenth century, ingenious American designers and gunsmiths developed a miracle weapon: the high-powered, large-caliber, long-range hunting rifle.

One pioneer of the category, the Hawken "plains rifle," also called a "buffalo gun" or "Rocky Mountain rifle," was made by the Hawken brothers of Saint Louis and was available in a half-stock version as a saddle weapon. With a thirty-to-thirty-eight-inch barrel, and a .53-to-.55-caliber ball, the Hawken had much better shocking power and knock-down power against a grizzly bear or buffalo than the .32-caliber American long rifle. Hunters, trappers, and prospectors heading west in the days of the California gold rush of 1849 loved the Hawken rifle. But the early versions were still flintlock-action muzzle-loaders, so you still had the problem of a very slow reload time versus a large charging animal.

Enter the Sharps rifle, a beautifully engineered, accurate, and sturdy shoulder weapon that packed a .54-caliber, 475-grain bullet with superb striking power. By the mid-1800s, percussion and breech-loading firing mechanisms were fast replacing the cumbersome flintlocks, and the Sharps was a prime beneficiary of the trend. The Sharps was perfect for the medium- and large-sized game west of the Mississippi. The bottom line was you could knock down a grizzly with a single well-placed round. Even though it was a single-shot rifle, a skilled operator could crank off nine or more shots a minute with it, since reloading was smooth and easy.

With a Sharps rifle, you could knock down a grizzly with a single well-placed round.

Gradually, the tide in the War Against the Grizzlies turned. Armed with Hawkens, Sharps, and the new Winchester and Remington repeaters that followed after the Civil War, mankind eventually vanquished the grizzly.

———————

BEFORE THE WAR WAS OVER, however, there was one grizzly bear who went on a bloody rampage around Colorado that lasted some thirty years.

He may have been the meanest, most powerful, and most feared grizzly bear in American history. He owned the mountains, and his reign of terror was supreme.

His name was Old Mose. He was so nicknamed because folks who caught fleeting glimpses of him in action said he shuffled along in a kind of "moseying" way. But don't let the cute nickname fool you; he was a man killer and a cattle thief.

Now, don't get me wrong. I've got nothing personal against Old Mose or any other grizzly, and generally speaking, grizzlies will leave humans alone as long as the humans stay out of their way. And after all, when a grizzly eats a sheep or a cow, they're doing what comes naturally; that's just how God programmed them.

But this bear stood out. First for his immense size—he was over twelve hundred pounds, and his huge body measured ten feet four inches long from nose to tail; second for the scale of the outrages he was blamed for and the total inability of anyone to stop him. The bear was accused of killing some eight hundred cattle, a number of horses, and at least three men. One cowboy watched as Old Mose chased down a three-year-old bull, slapped him around, flipped him over, and then sank his teeth into the target's neck for an instant kill bite. Another witness reported he saw the beast take down a running horse with a single paw swipe, then kill it with one chomp to the neck. Sometimes, witnesses testified, Old Mose would spy on lonely prospectors up in the hills, pop out in front of them, rise up, and let out a hellish growl. The victim, scared nearly to death, would flee in terror as the bear seemed to enjoy himself immensely. The bear absorbed at least twenty rounds of gunfire over the years, but he just kept on killing.

In 1886, an experienced bear hunter named Jack Ratcliff rounded up a posse, picked up Old Mose's trail, and tracked him for ten days. One day, Ratcliff spotted his quarry's den but slipped down a gulch, right into Ole Mose's kill zone. The bear lunged at Ratcliff from twenty-five feet; the hunter fired at and missed the bear, whereupon the grizzly tore Ratcliff's scalp off. Ratcliff's partners drove the bear off with gunfire, rescued the victim, and tried to carry him to safety, but it was too late. Ratcliff's dying words were "Boys, don't hunt that bear."

Ratcliff's dying words were, "Boys, don't hunt that bear."

Old Mose's hunting grounds ranged over seventy-five miles across both sides of the Continental Divide, and when he tired of one spot, he'd just mosey over to the next county for a while. Some thought he spent most of his time on Black Mountain in between Hartsel and Salida, and over time he was reported to show up on Pikes Peak and near South Park and Cañon City.

Some people thought Old Mose was a legend, just a combination of several other bears whose exploits over the years became conflated.

For years, a $500 reward was posted for Old Mose, to no effect. One old-timer named C. W. Talbot remembered,

The stockmen and the ranchers in this country were in terror of their lives on account of this big, three-toed bear. He ran the cattle ranges without a man's hand raised against him—they were all afraid of the monster. Even this big reward didn't bring out any hunters that were anxious to run foul of him. There were two or three men that had gone to the hills to look for him—and they never returned, and their bodies were never recovered—this was the reason that the scattered residents of the Antelope country were afraid to go into the hills for him. He pulled down cattle wantonly, destroyed calves and colts, tore down fences, chased the people who lived in the country and conducted himself as an outlaw and degenerate. He carried on this reign of terror for several months, and then disappeared from his usual haunts—and I tell you that there was a feeling of relief in this section when he left.

Then one day in 1904, thirty-five years after the rampage began, a hero arrived on the scene, in the form of a famous hunter and trapper from Idaho by the name of James Anthony, plus his four hounds, named Ray, Ring, Ginger, and Dummit, and a local rancher and guide with the unfortunate name of W. H. "Wort" Pigg.

At four o'clock on the afternoon of April 30, 1904, Old Mose finally met his match on the north end of Black Mountain, north of Cañon City, when, after many weeks of tracking the notorious beast, James Anthony directed his powerful, barking hounds to surround him. The bear didn't seem to mind.

"Now, what in thunder is that old fellow figuring on?" grumbled Anthony. "Never in my life did I see such an attitude of utter indifference by any bear towards my dogs."

Anthony raised his carbine and aimed for a neck shot. "I'll just take a shot," he murmured, "lemme see—about eighty yards."

Blast—a round of soft-nosed .30-40 penetrated near the bear's throat, but Old Mose was more preoccupied with the dogs that were yapping around him in a circle. "Too low," muttered Anthony, "darn that dog that was in the way."

He fired again and a bullet passed through Mose's shoulder, but the bear just glanced at him and went back to watching the dogs almost bemusedly. A third shot sent splinters into the bear's face from a nearby aspen tree, causing him to get up and move toward Anthony. A fourth shot hit him in the shoulder. The bear seemed to look around the countryside, as if sensing this was the last time he'd ever see it. After two more shots, the bear died, without so much as a moan or whimper.

When the carcass of the king of the grizzlies was strung up in Cañon City, the crowd swelled to over two thousand people. His

American bear hunt (LIBRARY OF CONGRESS)

remains rest in a climate-controlled locker on the University of California's Berkeley campus, as part of the school's Museum of Vertebrate Zoology mammal collection.

The War Against the Grizzlies, which began with the arrival of white explorers and settlers after 1810, lasted until 1910—just a few years after Old Mose's passing—by which time the grizzly bear was eliminated from about 98 percent of its original habitat on the North American continent.

By 1975, the population had dwindled so severely outside Alaska that the grizzly was added to the endangered species list.

In hunting, the finding and killing of the game
is after all but a part of the whole.
The free, self-reliant, adventurous life,
with its rugged and stalwart democracy;
the wild surroundings, the grand beauty of the scenery,
the chance to study the ways and habits of the woodland creatures—
all these unite to give to the career of the wilderness hunter
its peculiar charm.

—Theodore Roosevelt, *The Wilderness Hunter*

CHAPTER 7

MASTER HUNTER IN THE WHITE HOUSE

O ne day in 1907, the president of the United States decided to come down to Robertson family territory in Northeast Louisiana to do some hunting.

The president had heard that some bears were still roaming wild in the woods of Louisiana, and he wanted to hunt them. He had the toughest job in the world, and who can blame him for wanting to get out of the White House, blow off some steam, breathe in some sweet natural air in the bayou wilderness—and do some hunting.

He wanted to get real close to nature. And I can't think of a more beautiful place to do that than in my neck of the woods.

So the president packed up his guns, ammo, and gear and traveled to the Tensas Bayou in Northeast Louisiana, to a spot not far from where my house is now in West Monroe. It's about a twenty-minute drive from here. Back then, of course, there was much more wilderness around these parts.

The only trouble was, there were no bears to be found. For days and days, the president wandered the woods and swamps looking for some sign of a bear—a footprint, a glimpse, a rumor, anything. No luck. The chief executive was dejected, and rightly so.

Then, three days before he was scheduled to take a train back north, he heard the words he'd been waiting for. They were, in effect:

Shhhh . . . There's a bear nearby!

And he's coming toward us.

Wait, there he is!

This president was the greatest hunter in American history—and the greatest conservationist.

He was a short, sickly, nearsighted boy from New York City who grew up to become a war hero and a Nobel Prize–winning president of the United States.

His name was Theodore Roosevelt.

In the White House, he slept with a pearl-handled Browning Model 1900 .32 semiautomatic pistol on his nightstand, and he kept a rhinoceros head hung over the fireplace of his Long Island estate, next to elk and antelope heads. He probably hunted more different types of big game in more parts of the world, and did more to preserve America's wildlife and natural heritage, than any other American.

America's chief hunter, Theodore Roosevelt, 1885
(LIBRARY OF CONGRESS)

If you measure the impact of a man by the mark he leaves on his world, then few hunters and few nature-loving citizens can compare to Teddy Roosevelt. He literally reshaped America by spearheading the drive for conservation, and he left it behind a better land than when he found it.

I've always been fascinated by Roosevelt—his passions and his achievements—as hunter and as a man.

He was born into a family of blue-blooded New York City aristocrats in 1858 when much of America was still rich with wild game and Native American tribes still enjoyed many of their original hunting grounds. His boyhood heroes were Daniel Boone and Davy Crockett.

As a boy, Roosevelt fell in love with the outdoors and the study of nature, plants, animals, and insects, partly because fresh air helped relieve his asthma, but also for reasons he just couldn't explain. He recalled, "Certainly, I could no more explain why I like 'natural History' than why I like California canned peaches. . . . All I can say is that almost as soon as I began to read at all I began to like to read about the natural history of beasts and birds."

AMERICAN SPORTING SCENE: SNIPE SHOOTING.

Game-bird hunting, circa 1870 (LIBRARY OF CONGRESS)

When he was nine, Roosevelt wrote a pamphlet titled "Natural History of Insects," and his bedroom was stuffed with various animal specimens in a private collection he called the Roosevelt Museum of Natural History. "The collections were at first kept in my room," he remembered, "until a rebellion on the part of the chambermaid received the approval of the higher authorities of the household and the collection was moved up to a kind of bookcase in the hall upstairs." Author Candice Millard wrote that "as a boy, he filled his house and pockets with spiders, mice and snakes, studying and sketching them with discipline and talent that far exceeded his age." At the age of fourteen, he donated a bat, a turtle, twelve mice, and the skull of a red squirrel to the collection of the American Museum of Natural History in New York City.

As an adult who pursued a double life as East Coast politician and real-life Western hunter-cowboy, Roosevelt went on a long writing streak and produced a series of articles and several books about his hunting adventures and observations, including *Hunting Trips of a Ranchman*, *Ranch Life and the Hunting Trail*, "In Cowboy Land," and *African Game Trails*.

Roosevelt loved the West so much that he bought a fancy wardrobe of tailor-made hunting clothes, complete with what he described as "fringed and beaded buckskin shirt, horse hide chaparajos or riding trousers, and cowhide boots, with braided bridle and silver spurs." In 1883, at age twenty-five, he invested in the Maltese Cross and Elkhorn, two ranching operations near the Little Missouri in the Dakota Territory.

Life in the rugged wilderness changed the city boy forever. "He craved once more to be alone with nature," reported naturalist John Burroughs, "he was evidently hungry for the wild and aboriginal—a hunger that seems to come upon him regularly at least once a year, and drives him forth on his hunting trips for big game in the West." Roosevelt's cousin Nicholas wrote that Roosevelt took delight in the "apparently pathological extremes" of his adventures in the Dakotas, with "rides of seventy miles or more in a day, hunting hikes of fourteen to sixteen hours, stretches in the saddle in roundups of as long as forty hours." Roosevelt declared simply, "I owe more than I can ever express to the West."

In the early summer of 1884, Roosevelt set off on a hunting trip to the Badlands of the Dakota Territory, in part to escape the devastating grief he suffered because earlier that year, his young wife had died in childbirth, on the same day his mother died.

"I have been fulfilling a boyish ambition of mine—that is I have been playing at frontier hunter in good earnest."
—TEDDY ROOSEVELT

After the trip, Roosevelt wrote a letter to his sister, Anna, back in New York in which he revealed his love for hunting as a way of communing with nature and with solitude:

I have been fulfilling a boyish ambition of mine—that is I have been playing at frontier hunter in good earnest, having been off entirely alone, with my horse and rifle, on the prairie. I wanted to see if I could not do perfectly well without a guide, and I succeeded beyond my expectations. I shot a couple of antelope and a deer—and missed a great many more. I felt as absolutely free as a man could feel; as you know, I do not mind loneliness; and I enjoyed the trip to the utmost.

He added,

One day I would canter hour after hour over the level green grass, or through miles of wild rose thickets, all in bloom; on the next I would be amidst the savage desolation of the Bad Lands, with their dreary plateaus, fantastically shaped buttes and deep winding canyons. I enjoyed the trip greatly.

Later that year, Roosevelt went on a monthlong hunting trip to the Bighorn Mountains of the Wyoming Territory. He packed up a serious arsenal of firepower—a .40-90 Sharps Borchardt single-shot rifle, a .45-75 Model 1876 Winchester repeating rifle, a .50-150 Webley Express double rifle, and twelve hundred rounds of ammo. "I shall feel able to face anything," he wrote.

He was looking for elk, but he came across his first grizzly bear instead, and it was an experience he never forgot. "We had found where he had been feeding on the carcass of an elk; and followed his trail into a dense pine forest, fairly choked with fallen timber." Roosevelt recalled, "Cocking my rifle and stepping quickly forward, I found myself face to face with the great bear, who was less than twenty five feet off—not eight steps." Roosevelt described what happened when the creature turned his huge head toward him: "I could see the top of the bear fairly between his two sinister looking eyes; as I pulled the trigger I jumped aside out of the smoke, to be ready if he charged; but it was needless, for the great brute was struggling in the death agony, and, as you will see when I bring home his skin, the bullet hole in his skull was as exactly between his eyes as if I had measured the distance with a [carpenter's] rule." The bear, Roosevelt's first, was almost a thousand pounds and nearly nine feet long. He went on to kill many more.

For several years, Roosevelt lived the life of a hunter and rancher in the dying days of the Old West. He lived in the saddle, drove herds of cattle, broke and rode wild cow ponies, got in a saloon bar fight (he won with a punch that flattened his opponent on the barroom floor), and captured two cattle-rustling desperadoes and transported them to jail in subzero temperatures. When he bagged a specimen of big game, he often danced a victory jig to celebrate.

Through it all, Roosevelt savored the pleasures of sleeping under the stars, hunting for food, and exploring in the wilderness. He wrote,

There are no words that can tell the hidden spirit of the wilderness, that can reveal its mystery, its melancholy, and its charm. There is delight in the hardy life of the open, in long rifle in hand, in the thrill of the fight with dangerous game. Apart from this, yet mingled with it, is the strong attraction of the silent places, of the large tropic moons, and the splendor of the new stars; where the wanderer sees the awful glory of sunrise and sunset in the wide waste spaces of the earth, unworn of man, and changed only by the slow change of the ages through everlasting time.

But the brutal winter of 1886–87 wiped out most of his cattle and made Roosevelt realize how quickly the wildlife of the West was vanishing.

In 1889, while hunting in the Bitterroot Mountains, Roosevelt had one of his most dangerous showdowns with an animal, when he came across a grizzly bear close to his camp, lumbering toward him. He raised his .45-90 Model 1886 Winchester lever-action rifle and fired a round that pierced the beast's lung.

The bear let out a roaring, moaning grunt, and Roosevelt raced down the hill to cut him off.

I heard him utter a peculiar, savage kind of whine from the heart of the brush. Accordingly, I began to skirt the edge, standing on tiptoe and gazing earnestly to see if I could not catch a glimpse of his hide. When I was at the narrowest part of the thicket, he suddenly left it directly opposite, and then wheeled and stood broadside to me on the hill-side, a little above. He turned his head stiffly towards me; scarlet strings of froth hung from his lips; his eyes burned like embers in the gloom.

Roosevelt fired again, aiming for and hitting near the heart. He recalled,

Instantly the great bear turned with a harsh roar of fury and challenge, blowing the bloody foam from his mouth, so that I saw the gleam of his white fangs; and then he charged straight at me, crashing and bounding hard to aim. I waited until he came to a fallen tree, raking him as he topped it with a ball, which entered his chest and went through the cavity of his body, but he neither swerved nor flinched, and at the moment I did not know that I struck him. He came steadily on, and in another second was almost upon me.

> "The great bear turned with a harsh roar of fury and challenge, blowing the bloody foam from his mouth . . . and then he charged straight at me."
> —TEDDY ROOSEVELT

Roosevelt's Model 1886 Winchester repeater fired heavy rounds that were well suited for knocking down a grizzly, but this bear just kept on coming. And the hunter had another problem—he had come upon the bear with just four rounds in the rifle's tube magazine and only two shots were left.

Man and bear were now just inches apart.

Roosevelt fired a bullet straight into the bear's open mouth, shattering his jaw and entering the neck. But the bear just kept coming!

I'll let the great man himself tell you what happened next:

I leaped to one side almost as I pulled the trigger; and through the hanging smoke the first thing I saw was his paw as he made a vicious side blow at me. The rush of his charge carried him past. As he struck he lurched forward, leaving a pool of bright blood where his muzzle hit the ground; but he recovered himself and made two or three jumps onwards, while I hurriedly jammed a couple of cartridges into the magazine, my rifle holding only four, all of which I had fired. Then he tried to pull up, but as he did so his muscles seemed suddenly to give way, his head drooped and he rolled over and over like a shot rabbit. Each of my first three bullets had inflicted a mortal wound.

In 1902, while the forty-four-year-old Roosevelt was the twenty-sixth president of the United States, he went to Mississippi to hunt black bears. After three days, he couldn't find any. So his hosts caught an old 235-pound male with their hounds, tied a lasso around his neck, tied the bear to a willow tree, and called for Roosevelt to come along and shoot him.

Roosevelt took one look at the bear and angrily refused such un-sportsmanlike conduct, but he did order that the injured animal be put out of his suffering. The event became world-famous, and count-less millions of stuffed "Teddy bear" toys, originally inspired by Roo-sevelt's gallant image, have been sold around the world ever since.

In 1909, after leaving the White House, Roosevelt took his son Kermit and 250 porters and guides along on an epic 11-month, 2,500-mile safari through Africa, sponsored by the Smithsonian Institution. They trapped or shot over 11,000 animals, from insects and moles to hippos, elephants, and white rhinos. One rhino charged right at the former president as he and a colleague simulta-neously opened fire. "Before he could get quite all the way round in his headlong rush to reach us, I struck him with my left-hand bar-rel, the bullet entering between the neck and shoulder and piercing his heart," Roosevelt recalled. "Ploughing up the ground with horn and feet, the great bull rhino, still head toward us, dropped just thirteen paces from where we stood."

In 1914, Roosevelt attempted another epic trip, this time along South America's uncharted River of Doubt, but the trip was a slow-motion disaster, plagued by sickness, murder, and inferior boats and equipment. He succeeded in his historic mission to chart the river, but the trip nearly killed him, caused him to lose fifty-five pounds, and probably contributed to his early death at age sixty in 1919.

Theodore Roosevelt hunting in Africa, 1910 (LIBRARY OF CONGRESS)

With his writings, Roosevelt brought the excitement and drama of hunting to a national audience, and he revealed a sharp, sensitive eye for the romance of the American West and the personalities of different wild creatures. "There have been few days of my hunting life that were so full of unalloyed happiness as were those spent on the Bighorn range," he wrote. "From morning till night I was on foot, in cool, bracing air, now moving silently through the vast, melancholy pine forests, now treading the brink of high, rocky precipices, always amid the most grand and beautiful scenery; and always after as noble and lordly game as is to be found in the Western world."

Here is how Roosevelt described the whitetail deer:

In trotting, the head and tail are both held erect, and the animal throws out its legs with a singularly proud and free motion, bringing the feet well up, while at every step there is an indescribable spring. In the canter or gallop the head and tail are also held erect, the flashing white brush being very conspicuous. Three or four low, long, marvellously springy bounds are taken, and then a great leap is made high in the air, which is succeeded by three or four low bounds, and then by another high leap. A whitetail going through the brush in this manner is a singularly beautiful sight.

And the bear:

The lumbering, self-confident gait of the bears, their burly strength, and their half-humorous, half-ferocious look, gave me a real insight into their character; and I never was more impressed by the exhibition of vast, physical power, than when watching from an ambush a grizzly burying or covering up an elk carcass. His motions looked awkward, but it was marvellous to see the ease and absence of effort with which he would scoop out great holes in the earth, or twitch the heavy carcass from side to side.

And the elk:

Elk offer easy marks when in motion, much easier than deer, because of their trotting gait, and their regular, deliberate movements. They look very handsome as they trot through a wood, stepping lightly and easily over the dead trunks and crashing through the underbrush, with the head held up and nose pointing forward. In galloping, however, the neck is thrust straight out in front, and the animal moves with labored bounds, which carry it along rapidly but soon tire it out. Elk tongues are most delicious eating, being juicy, tender, and well flavored; they are excellent to take out as a lunch on a long hunting trip.

Roosevelt also wrote some passages I think capture the mysterious beauty of hunting better than anything I've ever read. Like this example, from his book *The Wilderness Hunter*:

No one, but he who has partaken thereof, can understand the keen delight of hunting in lonely lands. For him is the joy of the horse well ridden and the rifle well held; for him the long days of toil and hardship, resolutely endured, and crowned at the end with triumph. In after years there shall come forever to his mind the memory of endless prairies shimmering in the bright sun, of vast snow-clad wastes lying desolate under gray skies; of the melancholy marshes; of the rush of mighty rivers; of the breath of evergreen forest in summer; of the crooning of ice-armored pines at the touch of the winds of winter; of cataracts roaring between hoary mountain masses; of all the innumerable sights and sounds of the wilderness; of its immensity and mystery; and of the silences that brood in its still depths.

Teddy Roosevelt's lifelong experiences as a hunter and hands-on naturalist helped him become the greatest conservationist America has ever known. He cofounded the Boone and Crockett Club in 1887, which ever since has fought for "fair chase" ethical hunting, wildlife preserves, the founding of the National Wildlife Refuge System, the National Park and Forest Services, and landmark game laws like the Lacey Act in 1900, the Migratory Bird Hunting and Conservation Stamp Act in 1934, and the Pittman-Robertson Act in 1937.

Teddy Roosevelt's lifelong experiences as a hunter and hands-on naturalist helped him become the greatest conservationist America has ever known.

Roosevelt supported US congressional passage of the Yellowstone Game Protection Act in 1894, which prohibited the killing or trafficking of wildlife in the park. As president, he launched an unprecedented wave of habitat preservation and wildlife conservation measures and spearheaded the creation of state and federal bureaus that brought scientific principles to resource management. He set aside over 150 million extra acres in the national forest system. He created four game reserves, in Montana, Oklahoma, Arizona, and Washington. He established five new national parks and eighteen national monuments, and created the National Bison Range in Montana. He set aside the first fifty-one federal bird reservations, the first four national game preserves, and the first twenty-four federal irrigation projects.

Roosevelt's legacy can also be looked at in terms of sheer numbers. Jay Cassell of *Field and Stream* magazine once estimated that the number of white-tailed deer plunged from around thirty-four million, when the first white settlers came to North America, to fewer than five hundred thousand. In the late 1800s, elk and pronghorn herds were collapsing, passenger

White-tailed deer, Great Bay National
Wildlife Refuge, New Hampshire
(Greg Thompson,
US Fish & Wildlife Service)

pigeons were vanishing from overhunting, and you could barely find a wild turkey anywhere in the East.

But by the 1990s, after a century of wildlife stewardship first nationally championed by Teddy Roosevelt, wrote Cassell, "hunting opportunities abound across the United States," with white-tailed deer up to about 25 million, elks to 875,000, and turkeys to 4.2 million.

In his mission to protect American wildlife and wilderness, Roosevelt had the help of countless other American hunters and nonhunters, naturalists, and conservationists.

John James Audubon, hunter and naturalist
(LIBRARY OF CONGRESS)

One of his inspirations was John James Audubon, a renowned bird artist, ornithologist, and sport hunter who spent years wandering the American wilderness from Florida to the Rockies, hunting his own food and sketching birds and shooting them for specimens. The drawings in his masterwork book *The Birds of America* brought the beauty of nature to a mass audience and helped inspire Roosevelt's early thinking as a conservationist and naturalist. In 1843, while traveling along the Missouri River on a steamboat, he wrote to his brother-in law: "It is four days since we reached the country of elk, antelopes, buffaloes, wolves, wild cats and other sorts of varmints. Oh, dear fellow, that you were with us! How you would knock over all these animals! . . . The antelopes are beautiful small animals and run like the wind. We killed a black tailed [mule] deer, and finer venison I never ate. We have seen so many buffaloes that we pay little attention to them now. On our return they will be fat and good, and we will fire away upon them." Today, a leading conservationist group is named for him, the National Audubon Society.

One of Theodore Roosevelt's good friends, William Temple Hornaday, was an enthusiastic hunter who grew up on the Iowa prairie in the 1860s and played a big part in saving the buffalo. As a boy he gazed at vast formations of passing birds, and decided to become a naturalist and taxidermist. He went on hunting and specimen-gathering expeditions through North America and South America and Asia, was appointed chief taxidermist of the National Museum at the Smithsonian Institution in Washington, DC, in 1882, and launched the National Zoological Park in 1888.

Shocked at the disappearance of the buffalo, in 1889 Hornaday published *The Extermination of the American Bison*, which rallied popular support for the species, and he started the American Bison Society, which helped to eventually reestablish the nearly extinct western herd. In 1896 he was named director of the new Bronx Zoo and stayed there for the next thirty years as it became the leading zoo in America. Hornaday also launched the Camp Fire Club of America, which became a highly influential wildlife preservation group, and he and club members successfully lobbied to stop the hat industry in New York from killing birds to produce hats, to stop the indiscriminate killing of Pribilof fur seals in Alaska, reintroduce elks and antelopes and buffaloes in the West, to protect the Florida Key deer, and to enact the federal duck-stamp program, through which hunters for the last eighty years have helped preserve six million acres of wetland habitat by buying duck-hunting stamps.

Some folks just don't understand the contribution that hunters have made to rescuing and preserving the American wilderness and its wildlife. But old Teddy Roosevelt knew how important it was all along. To him, it was a sacred mission, and it turned out to be one of the greatest gifts an American has given to future generations. In 1905, while he was president, Roosevelt explained, "In a civilized and cultivated country wild animals only continue to exist at all when preserved by sportsmen. The excellent people who protest against all hunting, and consider sportsmen as enemies of wild life, are ignorant of the fact that in reality the genuine sportsman is by all odds the most important factor in keeping the larger and more valuable wild creatures from total extermination."

Teddy Roosevelt was living proof that hunters were the original conservationists. Conservation, environmentalism, sustainability—Theodore Roosevelt didn't invent these ideas single-handedly, but he gave them a power and force that no other American has managed to duplicate.

Why did Teddy Roosevelt and countless other hunters and fishermen become some of the greatest champions for protecting American wildlife and wilderness?

The answer is pretty simple.

They love it.

And that truth continues to this very day.

Thanks, Teddy.

———

LET'S GO BACK to the time when Roosevelt came down to Robertson family country.

On this 1907 hunt in Northeast Louisiana, Roosevelt met one of the last full-time mountain men in America, a legendary character named Ben Lilly.

Lilly was a professional hunter who was hired by stockmen and the federal government to track down and kill hundreds of black bears, cougars (a.k.a. mountain lions), and grizzlies all across the mountains, plains, and forests of the West and Southwest. He was re-

Ben Lilly
(LOUISIANA ENDOWMENT
FOR THE HUMANITIES)

ported to have killed some six hundred cougars in his lifetime, possibly the largest number credited to an American hunter. On a single expedition, Lilly was reported to have shot sixty-five bears in a Mississippi swamp. He wiped out most of the bears in a wide area of Louisiana.

Roosevelt hired Lilly as a guide for his Louisiana hunt and could hardly believe how tough the mountain man was. "The morning after we reached camp we were joined by Ben Lilley [sic], the hunter, a spare, full-bearded man, with mild, gentle, blue eyes and a frame of steel and whipcord. I never met any other man so indifferent to fatigue and hardship," Roosevelt recalled. "It had rained hard throughout the night and he had no shelter, no rubber coat, nothing but the clothes he was wearing and the ground was too wet for him to lie on, so he perched in a crooked tree in the beating rain, much as if he had been a wild turkey." Roosevelt watched the muscular, athletic, fifty-plus Lilly jump out of a barrel without touching the rim and reported that "he could run through the woods like a buck."

Lilly traveled with a pack of up to twenty-five hounds and fed them corn bread, raccoon, deer, and bear meat, and he rested his head on a dog as a pillow when he slept. One of the toughest and most effective hunters of the era, Lilly was quoted as saying, "Anyone can kill a deer, but it takes a man to kill a varmint," by which he meant a cougar or bear. "I am sure I improve in shooting all the time," he told a friend, "if a bear or lion ever jumps out of a tree and I am in sight, I will get three balls in it before it hits the ground."

Lilly was a devout Christian who was devoted to his Bible; avoided swearing, alcohol, and coffee; and never worked on Sundays. If his hounds chased a cougar up a tree on Sunday, he'd have them all stay put until Monday. His favorite outdoor food was cougar, and like the Apache, he thought that by eat-

Ben Lilly never worked on Sundays. If his hounds chased a cougar up a tree on Sunday, he'd have them all stay put until Monday.

ing the neck meat, the power of the wildcat was transferred into his own body.

On this bear hunt though, it looked like Roosevelt and Lilly, two of the greatest hunters in American history, would come up empty. "For several days we hunted perseveringly around this camp on the Tensas Bayou, but without success," recalled Roosevelt. "Deer abounded, but we could find no bear; and of the deer we killed only what we actually needed for use in camp."

Then, a few days before a disappointed Roosevelt was scheduled to go back to Washington to resume being president, he managed to track a bear, and he hurried to a spot where he thought they could ambush her, as the hounds chased her through the canebrake. He described the scene: "Peering through the thick-growing stalks I suddenly made out the dim outline of the bear coming straight toward us; and noiselessly I cocked and half-raised my rifle, waiting for a clearer chance." Roosevelt fired once, sending a bullet through both of the bear's lungs and out at the opposite side. He fired again, "breaking the spine at the root of the neck; and down went the bear stark dead, slain in the canebrake in true hunter fashion." It was a large, lean she-bear.

The president of the United States was delighted. Altogether, on the trip, Roosevelt and his friends bagged three bears, six deer, a wildcat, a turkey, an opossum, and a dozen squirrels, and they ate everything they killed except the wildcat.

At night, as the moon rose over the Louisiana bayou, Roosevelt and his hunting-mates enjoyed a ritual familiar to us in the Robertson family and to countless other hunters since time immemorial: "We sat around the blazing camp-fires, and, as always on such occasions, each hunter told tales of his adventures and of the strange feats and habits of the beasts of the wilderness."

I'll tell you a little secret.

Sometimes at night when I'm walking around our property, I can almost hear old Teddy's high-pitched laughter bellowing through the cooking smoke from across the hollows and pines, just a bit farther over there in the woods.

Nature does not care whether the hunter
slay the beast or the beast the hunter;
she will make good compost of them both,
and her ends are prospered whichever succeeds.
—John Burroughs, *Birds and Poets*

CHAPTER 8

THE HUNT THAT WENT OUT OF CONTROL

There was one hunt that shaped our nation more than any other—and it was the biggest hunt in American history.

For more than twenty years, mankind unleashed staggering waves of firepower on an animal population that numbered in the tens of millions.

When it was over, the species had almost vanished, and the destiny of the United States had been changed forever.

It was a tale of guns and empire, in an age before conservation and animal stewardship, and it affected millions of animals—and people. No other time in human history has seen such a vast slaughter of game in a bloodbath without rules, seasons, or limits.

It was the Great Buffalo Hunt of the 1800s.

Let's travel back 140 years to see what happened . . .

ONE DAY IN 1875, a man with a mustache sat cross-legged on the ground on the Great Plains west of Kansas City.

He peered through the carefully calibrated twenty-power telescopic sight of his rifle; his finger hovered close to the trigger. It was so sensitive that a puff of cigar smoke could almost set it off.

The man was Frank H. Mayer and he was one of the best professional buffalo hunters in the business. Mayer and his fellow hunters were called "buffalo runners," even though they didn't run on the job. Most of the time they sat or kneeled perfectly still. In fact, this was called a "still hunt" or a "buffalo stand" because both hunter and prey sat or stood mostly still.

Still-hunting buffaloes with a Sharps rifle (JAMES HENRY MOSER, NATIONAL EXPANSION MEMORIAL, NATIONAL PARK SERVICE)

His sixteen-pound rifle was braced thirty inches above the ground on a pair of sticks made of hard wood, bolted together to provide a rest on which to lay the heavy barrel. His left hand held the sticks steady. If he fired the weighty rifle while flat on the ground, the reverberation would scare off his quarry; the elevated rests reduced that risk.

The scope revealed a sight that meant money in the bank for Mayer—a group of American bison, buffaloes, shuffling around the prairie, chewing on grass. The species numbered in the millions, in herds that ranged far across the Western half of the United States, in lands that are today the Dakotas, Montana, Wyoming, Nebraska, Kansas, Oklahoma, and parts of Texas and Colorado.

Which one should I shoot first? he wondered.

Mayer studied the herd carefully, judging its mood, anticipating its movements, and spotting the leaders to pick off.

There was a backup rifle lying on a nearby tarp, along with a cleaning rod and extra ammo cartridges in case he missed—which he rarely did—or in case of a hostile Native American attack. Before choosing his spot, Mayer had carefully studied the wind direction by scattering a few stalks of grass in the air. He wanted to be sure he was not downwind of the buffaloes; they had an excellent sense of smell. Once the wind direction was

There wasn't much that frightened Frank Mayer, but the prospect of a buffalo stampede was downright terrifying.

confirmed, he picked a shooting position three hundred yards from the target. Any closer would risk panicking the herd and causing a stampede; any farther out would reduce the odds of a kill.

There wasn't much that frightened Frank Mayer, but the prospect of a buffalo stampede was downright terrifying. He'd experienced a buffalo stampede once before, two years earlier, in the summer of August 1873, and he still had nightmares about it. It was one of the closest calls he'd ever had.

He was camped on the North Canadian River in what's now known as Oklahoma. It was a lazy, clear, cloudless day, and Mayer was flat on his back soaking up the sunshine. Then he heard it—a faint rumble, like a steady, far-off thunder. None of his crew, who were sitting or standing, could hear it. But he could, since his head was on the ground. He jumped to his feet.

"Buffalo stampede!" he hollered. "Coming straight this way! Turn the wagons broadside and get your rifles—quick!"

In no time, the noise increased to a roar. The earth quaked. Mayer sent his men to places where they could shoot from between the wagon wheels. Shells were frantically jammed into breeches.

"Concentrate your fire on a single point. Maybe we can split the herd so it will pass on both sides of the wagons," Mayer ordered.

"We had a solid phalanx of six good men and true," recalled Mayer. It was a couple thousand charging buffaloes versus six men toting four .50-70 needle guns, a 56-56 repeating carbine, and Mayer's .45-120 Sharps rifle.

Mayer directed the boys to hold their fire until the buffaloes were four hundred yards away. The creatures appeared as a rock-solid wall of flesh and Mayer's guts did a few somersaults. He rose up and fired, dropping one of them.

His team opened fire; more buffaloes fell to the dirt. A heap of buffaloes piled up at one spot, and Mayer remembered, "Over this the rear guard tumbled and sprawled until it looked as if it were raining buffalo. The herd began to split up at the first volley, scampering away diagonally from that heap obstacle. We kept right on firing as rapidly as we could, always at the objective point, until at last they split completely, going off in two directions and missing our wagons by a wide margin." In five minutes, they had split the herd's stampede by creating a pile of thirty-seven dead and wounded buffaloes.

"It was five minutes of high life, and I am glad I lived them," Mayer recalled, "But I never wanted a repeat on them, I'll tell you."

On this day, Mayer had in his hand a weapon he thought was the best killing machine in the business, "absolutely unsurpassed by any weapon known to man." It was a side-hammer Sharps .45-120-550 rifle. The caliber was .45, which meant the bore was 45/1000 in diameter; the powder load was 120 grains; and the lead slug it fired weighed 550 grains.

After the Civil War, gun technology had advanced by leaps and bounds, which helped the two thousand or so working buffalo runners like Frank Mayer ply their trade on an industrial scale. Gun manufacturers created designs like the new-model Sharps rifles that had the range, accuracy, and knock-down power to kill big animals like grizzlies in the mountains and buffaloes on the range. Self-contained metal cartridges were developed, like the robust .50-70 "Government round"—a cartridge containing a .50-caliber bullet fired by 70 grains of black powder. These cartridges finally put an end to the messy process of fiddling with powder, patches, and balls. The cartridge married together the primer, powder charge, and bullet in one brass or copper case. Easy-to-load breechloaders replaced the pain-in-the-butt muzzle-loaders.

Frank Mayer paid a lot of money for his Sharps—$237.60 to be exact, which, in 1875, he noted, "was a small fortune to tie up in two pieces of walnut, a heavy piece of octagonal steel with a hole down the middle, and a big side hammer that could be cocked in the coldest weather with mittens on." The rifle never let him down. It had "Sharps Special Old Reliable" stamped on the barrel. Some hunters carried the dependable rolling-block Remington buffalo rifle, but Mayer preferred the Sharps. He'd seen the Sharps lay down two hundred buffaloes with just two hundred shots, most of them at optimal distances ranging from three hundred to six hundred yards, and in the face of heavy winds at straight-on, fishtail, or full crosscurrents. He'd even seen a Sharps drop a buffalo in one shot from a thousand yards. "Is there any modern rifle, even the magnums, which could do that?" he wondered. "Show it to me if you find it, will you?"

Within arm's reach was his backup rifle, also a Sharps, this one a .40-90-420 that he'd picked up a few years back. A self-described "gun nut," Mayer considered it "as sweet as a piece of ordnance as you would ever see," a rifle that "would kill anything that walked on the American continent, including Indians, of which [his] Sharps had killed a few."

To tell you the truth, the Great Buffalo Hunt, which peaked from 1870 to 1878, wasn't much of a hunt at all. Back in those days, except for a number of enlightened Native Americans and a handful of white citizens, there was little idea of "fair chase," conservation, sustainability, or animal stewardship. Instead, this was industrial-scale animal processing, powered by the rifle and railroad. It was, in Mayer's words, "sheer murder," "a shameless, needless slaughter." But, he added, "It was also an inevitable thing, an

Hunters stampeding a buffalo herd (LIBRARY OF CONGRESS)

historical necessity." To buffalo runners like Mayer, it was business, pure and simple. That's why they were also called "market hunters." Mayer explained, "I was a business man. And I had to learn a business man's way of harvesting the buffalo crop. Their hides were worth $2 to $3 each, which was a lot of money in 1872. And all we had to do was take these hides from their wearers. It was a harvest. We were the harvesters." It was good, steady, year-round work.

As another hunter, William "Billy" Dixon wrote, "It was deadly business, without sentiment; it was dollars against tender-heartedness, and dollars won." Congress passed a measure in 1874 to place limits on buffalo killing, but President Grant wouldn't sign it into law. The killing continued and kept growing.

As he sat on the plain and squinted through his scope, Frank Mayer was riding the crest of a tidal wave of buffalo hunting that engulfed the Old West from the 1840s to the 1890s and reshaped the foundations of America. In a sense, such a huge slaughter may have been inevitable as white settlers pushed west, but it was a hunt that eventually grew completely out of control.

For the buffaloes, one of the most tragic things about the hunt was their simple brain. When buffaloes were being shot at from a few hundred yards by an assailant they couldn't clearly see, they just didn't process the fact that they should skedaddle.

Instead, they milled around the dead or wounded fellow buffaloes, especially if one was the "boss cow," the female leader of the herd, hypnotized by the smell of her blood. This allowed Mayer, a skilled market hunter, to slowly work his way through the herd one by one, aiming for the heart or neck, maybe two shots per minute, switching rifles to avoid overheating, and easily hit his quota of fifty buffaloes a day, the maximum number of hides his crew could process in the field. Mayer explained, "We based it really on the overwhelming stupidity of the buffalo, unquestionably the stupidest game animal in the world. Nature provided the buffalo with almost no protective equipment. His eyesight was poor. His hearing was not much better." He added, "He would not or could not fight, and all the pictures you see of a buffalo turning on the hunter are pure bunk."

The Sharps rifle could kill at such a long range that Native Americans called it the weapon that "shoots today, kills tomorrow." In one buffalo stand, Mayer killed 269 buffaloes with three hundred cartridges at a range of three hundred yards. Another hunter by the name of Orlando A. Brown dropped 5,855 buffaloes in two months in 1876, for an average kill of 97 per day. He went deaf in one ear from the constant blasting of his Sharps Big 50. The record for speed was claimed by Tom Nixon in 1873, when he made a stand on the headwaters of Bluff Creek, south of Dodge City, and killed 120 buffaloes in forty minutes, in front of witnesses no less.

By the 1870s, railroads were hauling 250,000 hides per year to the East Coast, where they were fashioned into hats, coats, and industrial products of all kinds. Additionally, buffalo meat was shipped around regionally to feed soldiers at army outposts and railroad workers helping push civilization westward.

By 1873, witnesses said you could leap on buffalo carcasses along the banks of the Arkansas River for a half mile without touching the ground. At dusk, they said, multitudes of skinned corpses glowed in the fading sun like the lights of a big city.

Besides his Sharps rifle, Frank Mayer had another killing machine on hand, and it was stuffed inside his pocket.

It was a suicide capsule.

The device consisted of a .40-caliber shell shoved inside a .45-caliber shell, with a thin glass tube nestled inside the smaller shell. Inside the tube was a white powder containing cyanide.

Two years earlier, when Mayer went on his first buffalo-hunting expedition, his experienced partner, a man called McRae, asked him, "Frank, have you got a poison vial?"

"Poison vial?" he asked. "Never even heard of one. What's its purpose?"

"To save your scalp."

"To save my scalp?"

"That's right."

McRae explained how he invented the poison vial. One day he came upon the body of a white wagon driver who had been stripped and scalped while alive, his privates cut off and fastened into his mouth with a sinew cord. Big pine splinters had been jammed in his flesh from his ankles to his chin until he resembled a hedgehog. The splinters were ignited at his feet, triggering a gradual upward flame that roasted him alive. His body was strapped to a tree trunk with his own wagon chains.

"No Indian will scalp a dead man," McRae explained, hence his invention of the poison vial. "Wouldn't you rather have a quick painless death from poison than a tortured lingering death like that teamster? Always carry this," he said, handing Mayer a sample. "Hydrocyanic acid," McRae explained. "If Indians seem fit to capture you, bite hard on the tube. It's sure medicine against scalping and torture."

> **"If Indians seem fit to capture you, bite hard on the tube. It's sure medicine against scalping and torture."**
> —McRae

From then on, Mayer always carried the vial when he was on the job. He never had to "bite the white," as they called it, but he heard of two other buffalo runners who did. "Their bodies had not been mutilated or even scalped after death," Mayer recalled.

After 1869, the transcontinental railroads doomed the buffalo just as surely as the Sharps and Remington rifles did. Not only did the trains efficiently haul buffalo hides back east, they literally plowed through big buffalo herds and split them into smaller and smaller formations.

Railroad passengers and crew shot buffaloes, both for fun and to try to clear them off the track. *Harper's Weekly* described the scene:

Nearly every railroad train which leaves or arrives at Fort Hays on the Kansas Pacific Railroad has its race with these herds of buffalo; and a most interesting and exciting scene is the result. The train is "slowed" to a rate of speed about equal to that of the herd; the passengers get out fire-arms which are provided for the defense of the train against the Indians, and open from the windows and platforms of the cars a fire that resembles a brisk skirmish. Frequently a young bull will turn at bay for a moment. His exhibition of courage is generally his death-warrant, for the whole fire of the train is turned upon him, either killing him or some member of the herd in his immediate vicinity.

Another journalist, for *Harper's New Monthly Magazine*, reported: "It would seem to be hardly possible to imagine a more novel sight than a small band of buffalo loping along a railroad train, while the passengers are engaged in shooting from every available window. An American scene, surely."

Some think the buffalo hunt had an extra, evil purpose encouraged by forces in the US government: to conquer the Native Americans by exterminating the buffalo.

In addition to putting food on the table for thousands of railroad workers and frontier soldiers, and providing an income for buffalo runners like Mayer who sold buffalo products into the market, some think the buffalo hunt had an extra, evil purpose encouraged by forces in the US government: to conquer the Native Americans by exterminating the buffalo.

Frank Mayer reported that one day, while picking up free ammunition from an American military post in the West, a high-ranking officer explained, "Mayer, there's no two ways about it: either the buffalo or the Indian must go. Only when the Indian becomes absolutely dependent on us [white settlers and the US government] for his every need, will we be able to handle him. He's too independent with the buffalo. But if we kill the buffalo we conquer the Indian. It seems a more humane thing to kill the buffalo than the Indian, so the buffalo must go."

But Frank Mayer didn't think much about politics or strategy when he hunted buffaloes; he focused mainly on logistics.

Mayer carefully lined up his shot and gently pulled on the trigger, aiming at a target in the middle of the herd of some thirty

Shooting buffaloes on the Kansas Pacific Railroad line (LIBRARY OF CONGRESS)

buffaloes. The bullet hit the boss cow directly in the lungs and slammed her flat on the ground. It was a one-shot kill, the kind he specialized in. Some members of the herd perked up slightly, slowly milling around the corpse and pawing the ground, mesmerized by the scent of blood, and others paid no attention.

Mayer fired again and again, working his way slowly around the herd. More and more buffaloes dropped, until he hit his quota of fifty for the day. He mounted his horse and reported back to the boys, who were holding position off in the distance. They hitched up and moved the camp to the three-hundred-square-foot kill zone. Following the caste system of the buffalo range, Mayer relaxed, lay back, and had a smoke, while the skinners went about their grim, bloody work, swatting flies while plunging butcher knives into buffalo carcasses.

After the skinners were finished, more workers arrived at the stench-ridden killing field, men whom Mayer described as a "mean, ugly, cheap breed of drunkards" and a "grotesque wave of men." They were the "wolfers," who laced the buffalo carcasses with strychnine to kill the wolves and coyotes who flocked to the scene after a kill. A lot of buffaloes were skinned for their hides, their meat left to waste. Then the "boners" came; they collected the bones to be shipped east to be processed into fertilizer.

If you multiply the quota of fifty buffaloes he took in a day by about ten million, you will get an idea of the scale of the Great Buffalo Hunt of the 1800s. But for Frank Mayer, it was all in a day's work.

AT TEN A.M. on the chilly morning of January 12, 1872, a summit meeting happened at the North Platte train station on the Great Plains of Nebraska—featuring three of the most famous figures in American hunting.

The occasion was a visit by a member of the Russian royal family, a friendly young guy with mutton-chop whiskers named Grand Duke Alexis, the third son of Emperor Alexander II and Empress Maria Alexandrovna. He wanted to go hunting. To celebrate his twenty-second birthday, he wanted to jump on a horse, plunge into the wide-open spaces with a rifle in his hand, shoot buffaloes, and sleep under the stars.

Three Americans were waiting for Grand Duke Alexis as he stepped off the train from Denver.

The first man was General George Armstrong Custer, the flamboyant Civil War hero and Native American fighter who was also a hard-core wild-game hunter. He took a pack of hunting dogs with him wherever he went so he could peel off and do some hunting in his spare time.

In one letter Custer bragged, "I have done some of the most remarkable shooting . . . and it is admitted to be such by all."

Custer liked to write letters filled with hunting stories to his wife, Libbie, which would reach up to 120 pages. In one letter he bragged, "I have done some of the most remarkable shooting . . . and it is admitted to be such by all." He listed his kill: forty-one antelopes, four buffaloes, seven deer, four elks, a fox, and two wolves, plus prairie chickens, geese, ducks, and hens "without number." He learned how to perform taxidermy in the field and boasted, "I can take the head and neck of an antelope, fresh from the body, and in two hours have it fully ready for preservation."

Custer loved hunting animals because he thought it boosted his courage, his shooting, and his riding skills, and it reminded him of the "wild, maddening, glorious excitement" of the cavalry charges that made him famous in the Civil War. Behind his back, his men called Custer "Iron Ass," because he could spend all day in the saddle.

One day in 1867, Custer bolted far away from his Seventh Cavalry column to chase antelopes, spotted a big bull buffalo, and drew a bead on the creature's vital spot between the shoulders. The beast spun around and spooked Custer's Thoroughbred horse, causing Custer to fumble his gun and send a round into his own horse's brain, killing him and throwing Custer in the air.

The buffalo gave Custer a dirty look and sauntered off, leaving Custer deep in hostile Native American territory. On foot for hours, he managed to find his way back to his troops.

The second American on hand to greet the Russian duke was the notorious anti-Native American warrior and US army general Philip Henry Sheridan. He wasn't famous for his own hunting but for promoting the idea of slaughtering buffaloes as a way of vanquishing the Native Americans. He once publicly declared of the buffalo hunters,

> These men have done more in the last two years, and will do more in the next year, to settle the vexed Indian question, than the entire regular army has done in the last forty years. They are destroying the Indians' commissary. And it is a well known fact that an army losing its base of supplies is placed at a great disadvantage. Send them powder and lead, if you will; but for a lasting peace, let them kill, skin and sell until the buffaloes are exterminated. Then your prairies can be covered with speckled cattle.

When the Texas legislature tried to limit the hunt, Sheridan testified against it, arguing the buffalo hunters should be given medals instead.

The third American on hand to meet the Russian duke was William "Buffalo Bill" Cody, the legendary former Pony Express rider, mountain man, stagecoach driver, US Army Fifth Cavalry scout, and soon-to-be Medal of Honor winner who would become the most famous buffalo hunter of all time.

In an age when most folks thought it was impossible to exhaust natural resources, Cody mowed down buffaloes on a huge scale and earned his nickname after killing 4,250 bison in one year for the Union Pacific Railroad. Unlike buffalo stand-hunter Frank Mayer, Cody preferred "chase hunting" while mounted in the saddle of his horse, and he favored a .50-caliber trapdoor Springfield needle gun, not the Sharps rifle. His friend General H. E. Davies remembered that when the tall, striking-looking Cody was on the range, dressed in a fringed suit of light buckskin, a crimson shirt, and a wide sombrero on his head, "he realized to perfection the bold hunter and gallant sportsman of the plains."

Buffalo Bill (LIBRARY OF CONGRESS)

Buffalo Bill Cody volunteered to be Grand Duke Alexis's guide for the Nebraska hunt, and Custer and Sheridan pitched in to be hunting buddies on the excursion. This was a delicate moment in Russian-American relations; if the duke had a bad time hunting, it could set back diplomatic affairs between the two superpowers-to-be, which were frosty at the time. So the US government assigned Alexis a military escort of infantry, cavalry, and Buffalo Bill.

What happened next? Lucky for us, Buffalo Bill wrote it all down. He described what happened after Grand Duke Alexis was welcomed at the train station:

In less than half an hour the whole party were dashing away towards the south, across the South Platte and towards the Medicine; upon reaching which point we halted for a change of horses and a lunch. Resuming our ride we reached Camp Alexis in the afternoon. General Sheridan was well pleased with the arrangements that had been made and was delighted to find that Spotted Tail [of the Brulé Sioux] and his Indians had arrived on time. They were objects of great curiosity to the Grand Duke, who spent considerable time in looking at them, and watching their exhibitions of horsemanship, sham fights, etc. That evening the Indians gave the grand war dance, which I had arranged for.

Buffalo Bill reported that both General Custer and Grand Duke Alexis were in a randy mood. Custer flirted with one of Spotted Tail's daughters, and the duke had a crush on another Native American girl. "The night passed pleasantly," wrote Cody somewhat mysteriously, "and all retired with great expectations of having a most enjoyable and successful buffalo hunt. The Duke Alexis asked me a great many questions as to how we shot buffaloes, and what kind of a gun or pistol we used, and if he was going to have a good horse. I told him that he was to have my celebrated

Sioux hunter stalking buck, circa 1908 (Library of Congress)

buffalo horse Buckskin Joe, and when we went into a buffalo herd all he would have to do was to sit on the horse's back and fire away." Cody continued:

Of course the main thing was to give Alexis the first chance and the best shot at the buffaloes, and when all was in readiness we dashed over a little knoll that had hidden us from view, and in a few minutes we were among them. Alexis at first preferred to use his pistol instead of a gun. He fired six shots from this weapon at buffaloes only twenty feet away from him, but as he shot wildly, not one of his bullets took effect. . . .

Seeing that the animals were bound to make their escape without his killing one of them, unless he had a better weapon, I rode up to him, gave him my old reliable "Lucretia" [his trapdoor Springfield rifle, named after the femme fatale of the Borgia family], and told him to urge his horse close to the buffaloes, and I would then give him the word when to shoot. At the same time I gave old Buckskin Joe a blow with my whip, and with a few jumps the horse carried the Grand Duke to within about ten feet of a big buffalo bull.

"Now is your time," said I. He fired, and down went the buffalo. The Grand Duke stopped his horse, dropped his gun on the ground, and commenced waving his hat. . . . Very soon the corks began to fly from the champagne bottles, in honor of the Grand Duke Alexis, who had killed the first buffalo.

Grand Duke Alexis was so happy after he shot down his first buffalo that he grabbed Buffalo Bill in a Russian-style bro hug and kissed him, according to one eyewitness. On the second day of the hunt, the duke was so excited he began firing off rounds at the sky from his revolver, and everybody else joined in the fun, too.

By the end of the adventure, fifty buffaloes were dead, US-Russian affairs were improved, and Buffalo Bill was made even more famous, thanks to press coverage of the hunt.

Sitting Bull and Buffalo Bill (LIBRARY OF CONGRESS)

Later that year, the charismatic Cody began appearing in cowboy shows and he soon developed his own extravaganza, a circus-style production called "Buffalo Bill's Wild West." The show featured a cast of over 640 and a 37-piece cowboy band mounted on horses, and offered re-created battles with Native Americans, stagecoach stick-ups, sharpshooting demonstrations, and, of course, buffalo riding. It took fifty train cars to transport the show from city to city. The show made Cody a global superstar who performed for the Pope and Queen Victoria and befriended Teddy Roosevelt.

General Sheridan, ironically, went on to become a champion of preserving Yellowstone National Park, where the last of America's buffaloes were protected.

As for General Custer, well, we all know what happened to him in 1876 up in Montana Territory, at a spot called Little Big Horn.

In the 1840s, between thirty million and sixty million buffaloes still roamed freely across the continent, in herds so massive they earned the nickname "Thunder of the Plains." In 1842, one observer, Philip St. George Cooke, wrote: "Suddenly a cloud of dust rose over its [hill] crest, and I heard a rushing noise as of a mighty whirlwind, or the charging tramp of ten thousand horses. I had not time to divine its cause, when a herd of buffalo arose over the summit, and a dense mass, thousand upon thousand, galloped, with headlong speed, directly upon the spot where I stood. Still onward they came. Heaven protect me! It was a fearful sight."

As late as the 1870s, says historian E. Douglas Branch, "travelers along the Arkansas River passed through herds of buffaloes for two hundred miles, almost one continuous gathering." One reliable source, Colonel R. I. Dodge, said he saw a single herd that numbered around four million.

But the American buffalo-hunting frenzy rose to staggering proportions, and some sources estimate that four to five million were killed in 1872–74 alone, and only 20 percent or less by Native Americans. By the 1880s, the population was in free fall, and the hunting days of men like Frank Mayer were fast coming to an end. The final Lakota buffalo hunt occurred in 1882.

Some sources estimate that four to five million buffaloes were killed in 1872–74 alone, and only 20 percent or less by Native Americans.

Mayer clearly remembered the last buffalo he killed, up on the Musselshell River in Wyoming. "He was a pitiful object, old, decrepit, and sick," as Mayer told the story.

Already coyotes were around him, licking their chops in anticipation of the feed which would come, once he dropped, which he was sure to do very shortly. I saved him the trouble. I set the trigger on my old .40-90, aimed at his neck. It was just like old times, to have a buffalo in the stadia hairs, and maybe my heart leaped a little bit. I touched the delicate trigger, and the gun roared. He fell. He never knew what struck him. Nearby was a herd of twelve fine cows, all of which I could have easily killed. But I didn't even shoot one. My buffalo days were over. I had harvested the last of the crop.

Soon, Mayer recalled, it was all over: "One by one we runners put up our buffalo rifles, sold them, gave them away, or kept them for other hunting, and left the ranges. And there settled over them a vast quiet, punctuated at night by the snarls and howls of prairie wolves as they prowled through the carrion and found living very good. Not a living thing, aside from these wolves and coyotes, stirred. The buffalo was gone."

The destruction of the buffalo also marked the collapse of the Plains Indian culture that had thrived in America for some ten thousand years. Cut off from their sacred, life-sustaining buffaloes, the Native Americans could no longer be hunters, and they were pushed onto reservations. General Sheridan himself described the betrayal and destruction this way: "We took away their country and their means of support, broke up their mode of living, their habits of life, introduced disease and decay among them, and it was for this and against this they made war. Could any one expect less?"

In the hands of American market hunters, the Sharps rifles,

Remingtons, Winchester repeaters, and weapons like them played a huge role in American history. They came within a hair's breadth of eliminating the buffalo and grizzly bear. They put food on the table for countless thousands of American settlers, railroad workers, and families pushing west. And, by clearing the plains and prairies and nearly exterminating the buffalo, they had the tragic consequence of speeding up the fall of much of Native American culture.

By clearing the plains and prairies and nearly exterminating the buffalo, these weapons had the tragic consequence of speeding up the fall of much of Native American culture.

By the end of the 1800s, there were less than a thousand buffaloes left in America. But finally, the US Congress adopted measures to protect the buffalo, including prohibiting the killing of any animals in Yellowstone National Park, home to the only remaining buffalo population. Thanks to the emergency rescue efforts of conservationist-hunters and sportsmen like Teddy Roosevelt, and plenty of nonhunters, too, the American buffalo population was protected and slowly grew.

Today, the number of buffaloes has recovered to around five hundred thousand, thanks to decades of conservation. Plus, lots of folks have started realizing that not only is buffalo meat a healthy, protein-rich food, it tastes pretty dang good, too!

*Any woman who does not thoroughly enjoy
tramping across the country on a clear, frosty morning
with a good gun and a pair of dogs
does not know how to enjoy life.*
—Annie Oakley

*A woman in the earlier days
wasn't supposed to be a hunter.
Men looked at it as a men's club.
And now we're the fastest-growing segment
in the hunting world.*
—Mary Cabela

CHAPTER 9

THE RISE OF THE WOMEN HUNTERS

What was the greatest hunting day of my life?

It was the day my wife, Korie, came hunting with me.

In fact, it was the first time she'd ever been hunting in her whole life.

Not long ago, I got a call from my buddies Matt and Ryan Busbice, asking if I'd like to do some hunting at their lodge over in Olla, Louisiana, to cull some deer and help control the population.

"Sure, I'm in!" I replied.

The Busbice family are good friends and business partners of the Robertson family, and they make our Rut Hunter Deer Call and our Buck Commander Crossbow. They have beautiful property around their hunting lodge. It was early October, the start of archery season in Louisiana.

What was different about this trip was that unlike any other hunt I've ever been on, my wife asked if she could come along. She'd always been interested in the idea of hunting, but one way or another, with a family and many things to run, she'd just never made it out there with me on a hunt.

"Every year," Korie explained, "I think, *This is the year I'm going to start hunting.* This year, I just decided this was going to be the year."

I was super-excited to have her come out into the woods with me. I was a little nervous, too. I hoped she would enjoy the experience and not be disappointed. After all, it is the family business! I was really interested in taking her crossbow hunting, to show her how close you can get to the deer. It's about as close-up as you can get to hunting and to nature.

We were perched up in a tree stand twenty yards above the ground, just Korie and me, waiting for the deer with a crossbow with a telescopic sight. It was a two-man stand with a bench wide enough for two people to sit on.

Korie was all tricked out in full camo and face paint. She looked like the most beautiful jungle woman I'd ever seen.

Korie was all tricked out in full camo and face paint. She looked like the most beautiful jungle woman I'd ever seen.

The trouble was, she couldn't stop laughing. I had smeared face paint on her hands and face, and I guess my makeup job wasn't up to snuff. She looked at her face in the mirror and just cracked up. She couldn't believe my lack of cosmetic skills. "This is the worst makeup job I've ever seen!" she laughed.

"Shhh!" I said. "We can't hunt like this, you're going to scare all the deer off!" She understood and focused on the hunt.

Now, you've got to understand: Korie had never been in a deer stand before, she'd never duck-hunted, deer-hunted—nothing. Of course, she'd watched a lot of it on TV, but she really didn't have a clue about doing it in real life! We decided that I'd take down a really big deer if one appeared, and she'd go for a smaller one.

Well, we waited around for a deer for a while, and soon enough, a good-looking little six-point buck strolled into view, about seventy-five yards away. I thought, *Maybe Korie should shoot this deer.*

I handed her the crossbow, and I gave her a quick lesson on how to operate it.

"Here's all you gotta do," I whispered as softly as I could. "I'll take the safety off; all you gotta do is point, and . . . do you know where to hit it? Do you know where to hit the deer?"

She gave me the special kind of look that only a wife can give you and said, "Yes, I know where to shoot the deer—*I've watched your videos!*"

The deer looked right up at something. We froze perfectly still. For some reason it got spooked and scurried away.

"Take your finger off the trigger," I told Korie. "He's gonna come right back around, don't worry."

Lo and behold, after a while the deer came right back out and started poking around a few dozen yards away from our tree stand.

Korie was nervous, she later told me, but she also added, "I felt confident, too. I said to myself, *I think I can do this!*"

I whispered in her ear, "Okay, let's try to wait until he picks his head up. Take him when you're on him. You ready?"

She raised up and cradled the crossbow, leaned it carefully on the railing, peered through the sight, and aimed. She felt super-charged with excitement, but at the same time she was scared she was going to miss.

She pulled the trigger, and *boom*.

The arrow flew . . .

———

As long as there has been hunting, there have been women hunters.

As far back as thousands of years ago, some scientists reckon women hunted big game right alongside their men. Armed with stone-tipped spears, women hunters chased deer, horses, bison, and gazelles across Europe in male-female hunting teams, beating the bushes, blocking escape routes, and joining in the kill.

In Roman mythology, Diana was worshipped as the goddess of the hunt, wild animals, and the woods, and was a master of the bow and arrow.

Women hunters in Idaho, circa 1909 (OTTO M. JONES, LIBRARY OF CONGRESS)

In early American history, plenty of frontier women packed rifles, went out in the woods, and bagged turkeys, ducks, squirrels, or deer for the family dinner table, especially when their husbands were away on long hunting or trapping trips.

When US Army posts began popping up all over the West, some of the officers' wives went along on hunts and had a blast. One of them, Frances Roe, a lieutenant's wife, wrote, "I love army life here in the West, and I love all the things that it brings to me—the grand mountains, the plains, and the fine hunting."

It was in the late 1800s that American women hunters started really coming into their own. Let me introduce you to four of the most interesting such ladies—Medora von Hoffman, Ella Bird, Grace Gallatin Seton-Thompson, and Mary Augusta Wallihan.

They all had a few things in common. They were pioneer-women types, tough and strong, and were crack shots. They had the special insight, sensitivity, and skill of female hunters.

MEDORA VON HOFFMAN was the daughter of a wealthy New York City banker, and when she married the hot-tempered, French Marquis de Morès, she became known as Medora de Vallambrosa, the Marquise de Morès. In the 1880s the two lovebirds set off to live the frontier life in the Badlands of the Dakota Territory, where she became a hunting buff and accomplished horsewoman. She shot better than her ex-soldier husband, and she liked to kneel down and knock the heads off prairie chickens with rifle shots.

The Marquis and Marquise de Morès with horse and Winchester, circa 1884 (STATE HISTORICAL SOCIETY OF NORTH DAKOTA)

Medora also liked to take weeks-long hunting expeditions into the Black Hills and the Bighorn Mountains, and she traveled in style. Her tailored shooting costume and fur-lined coat cost $2,800 in today's currency. She had a custom-built wagon that held a parlor, a kitchen, bunks, and a bathroom. For shorter hunting trips she used a smaller wagon, this one a copy of the coach Napoléon used to travel to Moscow. The backseat flipped into a bed and the drawers were filled with fine silver sets.

On an 1885 trip to the Bighorn Basin, she spent $14,300, but it was worth it. She killed two black bears and two grizzlies. She left the West and moved to France after her husband lost most of his money on bad investments. She volunteered as a nurse in World War I and died from war-related injuries in 1921.

But I'd bet that Medora would most like to be remembered doing what she loved doing best back West—charging across the prairie with a smile on her face and a stylish eagle feather stuck in her hat, her gun nestled in the saddle.

———————

ANOTHER FINE FEMALE HUNTER of the period was Ella Bird. She was sixteen years old when she married a Texas Ranger in 1877 and she followed her husband to Comanche country in King County, Texas, on an isolated range one hundred miles west of Fort Griffin. There they lived off the land and camped in a buffalo-hide tepee while joining in the slaughter of the buffaloes. Ella's husband wanted her to shoot well, so he trained her on a Model 1873 Winchester repeater. She was an excellent student—before long she was hitting the heads off of prairie dogs. Another time she killed three roosting wild turkeys with a single shot.

When she and Mr. Bird headed off for the buffalo range, they packed some serious heat. They carried a big sixteen-pound Sharps .45 buffalo gun, several hundred five-inch cartridge shells, primers, a keg of powder, fifty pounds of lead, bracing sticks to prop up the gun, two skinning knives, and a Bowie ripping knife. Soon they were hunting together as a team, killing, skinning, and dressing buffaloes by day and savoring buffalo steaks at night in their tepee. It tasted so good they never got tired of it.

When her husband died in 1888, she stayed on the prairie, fed her family antelope and deer, and sold cowboy fashion items she made from skins to local ranchmen. She also shot wolves for bounty money.

Ella Bird became such a renowned huntress that cowboys flocked to her property in search of a date.

Ella Bird became such a renowned huntress that cowboys flocked to her property in search of a date. She waved most of them off with a firm display of her Winchester.

WHEN NEW YORK CITY GIRL Grace Gallatin married the famous nature writer Ernest Thompson Seton (whom she nicknamed "Nimrod," after the biblical hunter), she yearned to share her husband's passions for hunting, fishing, and the outdoors. So she followed him out to Wyoming's Teton range and learned to shoot.

She never forgot her first kill. "The sun was just dropping behind the great Tetons, massed in front of us across the valley," she wrote. "We sat on our horses motionless, looking at the peaceful and majestic scene, when out from the shadows on the sandy flats far below us came a dark shadow, and then leisurely another and another. They were elk, two bulls and a doe, grazing placidly in a little meadow surrounded by trees." Grace and her husband froze absolutely still.

"There is your chance," said Nimrod.

"Yes," she agreed, "here is my chance." The elk passed into the trees and the two hunters dismounted.

"There are seven shots in it," Nimrod declared, handing his wife his rifle. "I will stay behind with the horses."

Grace crept down the incline, trying to stay under cover in the setting sun. A single idea dominated her brain: "to creep upon that elk and kill him." She glided past the scrub brush and pine trees.

Then, suddenly, I saw him standing by the river about to drink. I crawled nearer until I was within one hundred and fifty yards of him, when at the snapping of a twig he raised his head with its crown of branching horn. He saw nothing, so turned again to drink. Now was the time. I crawled a few feet nearer and raised the deadly weapon. The stag turned partly away from me. In another moment he would be gone. I sighted along the metal barrel and a terrible bang went booming through the dim secluded spot. The elk raised his proud, antlered head and looked in my direction. Another shot tore through the air. Without another move the animal dropped where he stood. He lay as still as the stones beside him, and all was quiet again in the twilight.

Grace sat motionless on the ground where she had shot, absorbing the incredible stillness of the moment. "So that was all," she thought. "One instant a magnificent breathing thing, the next—nothing. Death had been so sudden." She had no regrets and no feeling of glory or exhilaration, just wonder at what she'd done, and a "surprise that the breath of life could be taken away so easily."

> "One instant a magnificent breathing thing, the next—nothing. Death had been so sudden."
> —GRACE GALLATIN SETON-THOMPSON

Her husband, alarmed at the long silence, scrambled down when he heard the shots.

"I have done it," she said in a dull tone, pointing at the carcass.

"You surely have," said Nimrod. He measured the distance at 135 yards. They examined the elk's remains.

"How beautiful his coat was," she remembered, "glossy and shaded in browns, and those great horns—eleven points—that did not seem so big now to my eyes."

"You are an apt pupil," Nimrod said to his wife, marveling. "You put a bullet through his heart and another through his brain."

"Yes," said Grace, "he never knew what killed him."

Another day, the couple tracked a group of antelopes for three hours across the plains. "We hid behind low hills, and crawled down a water-course, and finally dismounted behind the very mound of prairie on the other side of which they were resting, a happy, peaceful family. There were twenty does, and proudly in their midst moved the king of the harem, a powerful buck with royal horns.

"The crowning point of my long day's hunt was before me," wrote Grace. "That I should have my chance to get one of the finest bucks ever hunted was clear. What should I do, should I hit or miss? Fail! What a thought—never!" Suddenly the wind betrayed their scent to the animals, and the whole band took off "like a flight of arrows."

"Shoot! Shoot!" yelled Nimrod.

Grace already had the same idea; her rifle was trained on the flying buck, a hundred yards away. *Blast.* "The deadly thing went forth to do its work. Sliding another cartridge into the chamber, I held ready for another shot. There was no need. The fleet-footed monarch's reign was over, and already he had gone to his happy hunting ground. The bullet had gone straight to his heart, and he had not suffered."

Just as memorable to Grace were the many shots she did not take, the many times she just felt connected to nature. "Of the many, many times I have watched them and left them unmolested, and of the lessons they have taught me," she explained, "I have not space to tell, for the real fascination of hunting is not in the killing but in seeing the creature at home amid his glorious surroundings, and feeling the freely rushing blood, the health-giving air,

the gleeful sense of joy and life in nature, both within and without."

"The real fascination of hunting is not in the killing but in seeing the creature at home amid his glorious surroundings."
—GRACE GALLATIN SETON-THOMPSON

One time, in the Bitterroot Mountains, Grace found herself alone one night while Nimrod went off to deal with the horses. She sensed the presence of a giant animal passing over to the river to drink. It was a grizzly bear, barely forty feet away. She raised up the rifle. "How the glory of it would ring down through the family annals," she recalled "unaided, hand to hand, so to speak, [the] encounter of a monster and the wonderful heroism of the woman." She fired and missed the beast.

She described the poignant scene that unfolded:

The bear turned and started back toward the way he had come, evidently on a runway, he looked as big as an elephant; already another cartridge was jerked in. . . . I had the gun at the shoulder and then for the first time the creature, who was now a mastodon, saw me. Its little eyes glared straight at me. I shall never forget them, and there we stood, transfixed. For the fraction of a second he debated what to do and then turned slowly away. Now was the moment. There would have been no miss this time.

She lined up a direct shot to the bear's brain. "It was so close—my finger on the trigger! Then I lowered the muzzle to the ground—and let him go. He had refused to injure me! Could I do less?"

———————

THEN THERE WAS THE COLORADO HUNTRESS Mary Augusta Wallihan, part of another husband-wife team.

Wallihan grew up in Wisconsin watching her father drop partridges, ruffed grouses, and squirrels from the top of tall maple trees with rounds from his muzzle-loader, taking the head off every time. She remembered, "Many a time I sat by his side watching him mold the round bullets, thinking them so pretty and bright as they rolled out into the box that caught them. He could drop a black bear, a panther or wild cat. The panther of the east, the lion of the mountains, one and the same—the cougar or puma more properly."

Mary Augusta Wallihan, 1895, with a .40-70–caliber, Remington-Hepburn rifle and a mule deer (MUSEUM OF NORTHWEST COLORADO)

Rea

She went out to small-town Wyoming, then Colorado, where she and her husband, Allen G. Wallihan, ran a post office, roadhouse, and frontier weather station. With her husband's encouragement, she learned how to shoot, and she quickly graduated from a shotgun to her favorite Remington-Hepburn rifle. She discovered she loved hunting mule deer, antelopes, and elks so much that she and her husband went out shooting as often as they could in the 1880s and early 1890s, toting a huge early-model camera out in the sagebrush to take still pictures. The two pioneering wildlife photographers took so many stunning photos of frontier hunting that they published a picture-album book on the subject titled *Hoofs, Claws and Antlers of the Rocky Mountains*, with an introduction by none other than Teddy Roosevelt.

Augusta liked to wear beautiful dresses and keep her hair in sausage curls, and she took her beloved dog, Jack, along to fish and hunt. When she pulled in a big trout, Jack jumped out and grabbed the fish to bring it back to her.

One time, Augusta pulled off an extremely difficult maneuver: she killed two bucks with one shot. She wrote:

In the fall of 1891 my husband told me I must get the winter's meat while he took photographs of the deer. So we commenced in the usual way by saddling our ponies and starting out with rifle to kill the deer and camera to take the photos. The first day I got nothing. The second I lost a fine buck because I had to shoot past my husband, as I thought, too close for safety. Then I moved a hundred yards or more from him. I had hardly got ready before I saw two fine bucks and a number of does and fawns. I confess I was a little selfish—I wanted both bucks very much. As I had lost the large one I thought two with one shot would please my husband very much. So quicker than I can tell it I fired and killed them both at 130 yards with one shot.

An article in the *Rocky Mountain News* marveled that "there is no record in the annals of sportsmen" of such a feat. "She always takes deliberate aim," the article noted, "and very rarely misses."

One winter day, Augusta got a message from some friends on the White River: "Come over at once and you can get some lion pictures." There was a group of marauding cougars on the loose, and the ranchmen were furious as usual, as the mountain lions had killed up to 50 percent of their colts every season. Mary and her husband pitched in right away to help cull the lion population. After twenty-six days of exhausting hard work, stalking, tracking, and shooting in the cold mountains, Augusta and the boys got the job done.

Mary Augusta and Allen Wallihan were invited to show their wildlife pictures at the 1900 Paris World's Fair and at the 1904 World's Fair in Saint Louis. In their later years, the couple wrote for national sportsmen's magazines and newspapers, lobbying for responsible game management and for protection of the deer and elk herds from commercial overhunting.

In 1900, the couple wrote a stark warning in *Outdoor Life* magazine:

> I presume you are wondering how the deer are in Routt County [Colorado] by this time. I can tell you they are being hunted more than ever, and thousands are being slaughtered. I have been told that four large wagons have been loaded to go to Snake River, each wagon being drawn by four horses. This only gives an idea of what is going on. When men having plenty of cattle turn out to kill four-horse wagon loads of deer to take out of the country it is time to call a halt. We have but a few years left of deer-hunting in Colorado—that is very evident.

The great American hunter Mary Augusta Wallihan lived a long, adventurous life until she suffered a stroke in 1922 and died at her home. She was buried on a hill overlooking her property and the wide-open spaces she loved.

I think she'd be happy to see how many wildlife populations have rebounded and thrived across America ever since.

IN OCTOBER 1905, two women traveled by rail and steamboat to New York State's rugged Adirondack Mountains for a ladies' hunting trip.

They hiked sixteen miles through forest and mountains, stopped at a log cabin, and chowed down on flapjacks, bacon, and coffee prepared by their guides.

Bright and early the next morning, the women went out hunting. They soon spotted a fine buck with a nine-point rack. One of the hunters, Emma Preston, took a shot, but the deer bounded away, and Emma felt her heart sink. They found a blood trail, however, and the deer's carcass a few yards away. The guide, who toted the deer three miles back to the cabin, figured that it weighed 175 pounds. "To say I was overjoyed would draw it mildly," she explained. "My rifle had done its work well."

Emma Preston was like many other American women of the twentieth century who loved the outdoors and saw hunting as a birthright and pursued the sport alone, with their husbands, or with female companions.

Today, there is a powerful sisterhood of twenty-first-century female hunters thriving across America, and their ranks are steadily growing.

They include a number of incredibly skilled technical shooters, a group that was showcased

Today, there is a powerful sisterhood of twenty-first-century female hunters thriving across America, and their ranks are steadily growing.

by *Outdoor Life* magazine a few years back as having achieved world-class scores in the Safari Club International rankings.

Debra Card, for example, held the number one spot for Alaska-

Yukon moose for nearly a decade by taking an enormous 39-point bull near Cordova, Alaska, with a total rack score of 731⅛ inches and an outside rack spread of more than six feet. Barbara Sackman had no less than 191 animals in the SCI rankings, including Alaska moose, Nile crocodile, Cape buffalo, rhinoceros, hippopotamus, polar bear, African lion, and leopard. Her daughter-in-law Maryann Sackman earned 93 spots in the SCI trophy book, including mule deer, bighorn sheep, kudu, bongo, musk ox, and whitetail deer. Then-fourteen-year-old Caroline Pruitt had already scored 18 trophies in the SCI rankings using muzzle-loaders and handguns and before switching mostly to crossbow. In 2000, Julie Weigel of Wisconsin scored the tenth-ranked American mountain goat in Bigfork, Montana.

Colorado hunters, 1967 (LIBRARY OF CONGRESS)

Mary Cabela of Nebraska is another powerful force in American hunting. Inspired by her love of the outdoors and her fifty-plus-year marriage to her husband, Dick, she helped turn a mail-order fishing-supplies business that started on the family kitchen table into Cabela's, the number one hunting and outdoor retail company in the United States, valued at over $3.5 billion. Her passion for hunting has led her to remote areas of North America, South America, Africa, Asia, and Europe in search of adventure. For decades, the Cabela family has advocated for hunters and for wildlife conservation.

A number of female celebrities have publicly described their hunting connections, often established when they grew up in hunting families themselves. Country music legend Lorrie Morgan is a well-known hunting enthusiast. *Desperate Housewives* star Eva Longoria was raised on a ranch in Corpus Christi, Texas, where she learned to handle firearms as a girl, and her father hunted rabbits, deer, turkeys, quails, and wild pigs, all for the family dinner table.

"I'm a hunter," declared the camo-loving, Texas-born country superstar Miranda Lambert. She got a BB gun at age seven, trained on a rifle at around twelve, learned handgunning from her police-officer dad, and carries a gun on her tour bus.

"I mostly deer-hunt and turkey-hunt," Miranda explained to the Minneapolis *Star Tribune*. "Usually during deer season I try to take Mondays through Thursdays off for a couple of weeks to go hunting. I went down to Texas and I got a couple of deer, one with

Hunters in a blind (Paul Kerris, US Fish & Wildlife Service)

a bow and one with a rifle. My biggest one is a 145 last year [a point total based on antlers]. I've got some trophy mounts. The first deer I killed with a bow was like a terrible-looking, sick deer that needed to be taken away from the Earth. Bless its heart; it had been run over [by a vehicle]. But I killed it with my bow and I definitely kept the horns from that one."

On her album *Crazy Ex-Girlfriend*, Miranda Lambert sang, "I'm gonna show him what a little girl's made of: gunpowder and lead." Her father, Rick, explained, "Miranda has lived in gun culture all her life. I'm a firearms collector and hunter. She was taught to shoot when she was a little bitty girl. So it's natural for her to put a gun in a song." Miranda once listed all the important things she needed for hunting—a bow, camo, binoculars, a pink cup, and lip gloss. When she married fellow megastar Blake Shelton, Lambert served her wedding guests venison she'd harvested herself.

Jennifer Lawrence inspired countless women and girls around the world to take up archery after playing badass bow hunter and survivalist warrior Katniss Everdeen in the *Hunger Games* movie series. In 2012 *Rolling Stone* reported that she learned how to shoot rifles and gut a squirrel for her 2010 film *Winter's Bone*. "I should say it wasn't real, for PETA," she said of the squirrel. "But screw PETA." She added that she was "thinking about buying a house. And a big dog. And a shotgun."

> **Miranda Lambert once listed all the important things she needed for hunting—a bow, camo, binoculars, a pink cup, and lip gloss.**

Canadian-born Eva Shockey has also become an inspiration for young women hunters in America. With her father, she cohosts *Jim Shockey's Hunting Adventures* on Outdoor Channel and in 2014 she appeared on the cover of *Field & Stream* magazine, the first woman to do so since Queen Elizabeth and her hunting dogs in appeared in 1976.

Eva accompanied her dad on hunting and fishing trips ever since she was a little girl, but it wasn't until she was twenty years old that she first killed a deer herself, with a bow. She remembered how moving the experience was: "It was emotional, I was excited, I was nervous, I was worried. As a hunter, if you don't feel remorse, if you don't feel reverence for that animal that just gave you a life, then I think you maybe should rethink it, because that's an animal, that's a living animal, and it's now become food for people."

In 2014, when Shockey put a photo of herself on her Facebook page with a 510-pound black bear she had killed in Hyde County, North Carolina, she was criticized by some folks, even though it was perfectly legal and contributed toward controlling a fast-rising bear population that was causing extensive crop damage in the area. She publicly defended herself, explaining, "Obviously we're not gonna get rid of the humans . . . [so] you have to keep the bear population in check." Of the critics, she said, "They don't understand that we eat all that meat. I mean, what are they eating at their dinner table? Do they have meat on their plate? Do they go to Whole Foods and buy a $20 steak? Do they know where that steak came from?" She told Fox News, "I believe with every part of me that what I'm doing is right, so there's nothing that I'm apologizing for."

Shockey has become a role model for a new generation of responsible, ethical, and passionate American hunters. She told *Field & Stream* magazine, "The number of women I meet—young girls, teenagers, moms with babies, older women—who tell me they hunt or are taking up hunting is incredible." There are plenty of other great women hunters on TV as well, including ladies like Tiffany Lakosky, Vicki Cianciarulo, Nicole Jones Reeve, and Bonnie McFerrin.

Tiffany Lakosky, an accomplished bow hunter and cohost of an Outdoor Channel hunting show, recently explained, "Women are realizing how much fun hunting is and how close it can actually bring them in their relationships with their families. The whole concept is that I am shooting my family's dinner tonight and we're eating something I shot." She added, "We are all part of the food chain. There is a balance in nature. People go to the supermarket and they think that somebody's growing a TV dinner somewhere to feed them. They are just not connected to it like people were one hundred years ago."

"The whole concept is that I am shooting my family's dinner tonight and we're eating something I shot."
—TIFFANY LAKOSKY

On June 7, 2014, the *Wall Street Journal* reported that a new breed of "urban girl hunters" are traveling together to special hunting ranches in the western United States to shoot, gut, and cook organic game like elk, peccary, and pheasant. "If I eat bacon, I should live with the experience of slaughtering the hog," explained chef and former investment banker Georgia Pellegrini. "I am understanding the process from beginning to end, and feeling it intensely. And the meat tastes better if you have killed it yourself." She added, "Some women seek their inner hunter. Others just want a break, good company, and fresh food."

Janice Baer, the vice president of the Women Hunters online

forum, notes that hunting appeals to women who want to procure their own healthy, local meat. She explained to a reporter: "Wild game is naturally low in fat, and free-ranging animals have no hormones that have been added to their diet. We know exactly what we're getting when we harvest our own food."

Cadi Thompson is a twenty-five-year-old hunter from Mississippi, and she believes that women bring special strengths to the sport. "Girls hunt differently than guys, and in some ways we're better," she explained. "We're more careful with gun safety. We don't drink while we hunt. A lot of guys don't care about killing a doe with a fawn." But she won't. "Girls are less competitive than guys when they hunt," she argued. "We're more supportive of each other." Cadi has hunted white-tailed deer since she was seven years old and favors a .243-caliber rifle, what she calls a "girl gun," with light recoil but enough punch to take down a deer. Like many other Southern women, Cadi enjoyed lots of hearty-tasting venison while growing up, and her favorite family recipe is grilled "deer-meat poppers," made with cream cheese, jalapeño, and bacon.

Cadi's friend and fellow young hunter Amber McMillen smiled after she killed a big eight-point buck with lots of meat on him. "My family doesn't hunt, and they don't really think girls should hunt, but they love to eat deer sausage," she noted. "I'll take him to the processor and get a ton of sausage made. They'll be happy when I bring it home."

Today, over 19 percent of hunters in the United States are

women, and their numbers are growing fast. The National Sporting Goods Association estimated a nearly 43.5 percent increase in female hunters from 2003 to 2013, up to almost 3.35 million. It's no wonder that businesses are rushing to cater to them—a 2011 Census Bureau survey calculated that female hunters spend $4.2 billion a year on hunting gear and clothes, or $2,800 a year on average per person. Some 30 percent of the goods in outdoor stores and hunting catalogs are now geared to women, and clothing, guns, and gear are being improved and specially modified for the rising new breed of women hunters.

WHAT HAPPENED ON THAT DAY when my wife, Korie, let that arrow fly?

At first I wasn't exactly sure, but it looked like a kill to me. The deer jumped and shot off a ways toward the west.

Korie and I climbed down out of the tree stand, found the blood trail, and followed it several dozen yards into the woods. In a minute we found the deer carcass. I froze in my tracks.

"*Look at this shot!*" I yelled.

I was awestruck. I just could not believe what a perfect shot my wife had made. It was a precise bull's-eye hit through the heart and out the other side, a clean, instant kill. We found the arrow stuck in a nearby tree.

Absolutely incredible. This was the first time Korie had gone hunting in her life and the first shot she had ever taken! We hugged hard and laughed hard, and she seemed overjoyed at what she'd done.

"That's a cull right there," I said. "This is going to be good eating!"

She proudly inspected the deer and said, "I'll take him."

I don't know if I've ever felt like that in a deer stand. I couldn't have been more proud of her. This was her first hunt ever, and she rose up and shot a deer right off the bat. I felt better than if I'd done it myself. I try not to get too emotional with my kids and my wife, but I was so proud she could experience this and see it firsthand that I got tears in my eyes.

Korie remembers her first hunt this way:

I loved the whole experience—it was an adventure!

Willie and I sat in the deer stand, with no distractions, no cell phones, no TVs or other people. It was really nice. The plan was if a really big deer came by, Willie would kill it, because I didn't want to miss or injure it.

Then the perfect deer appeared. I had practiced with the crossbow, and when I saw it I felt really confident.

Willie said, "Do you know what you're doing?"

I felt like I did. I'd seen all of Willie's deer-hunting videos, so I knew where I was supposed to aim and what I was supposed to do!

"Are you sure?" asked Willie.

"I'm sure!" I whispered.

I had the heart of the deer right in the crosshairs. As soon as I took the shot I started shaking—and in videos I've seen many people start shaking after they kill a deer. I always wondered why they did it. It's an adrenaline buzz—you're so focused on that one moment, and making sure you get it right, that once it passes your body just can't help shaking.

It was a perfect shot, a good, clean shot. The deer jumped and went thirty feet, not far at all, and dropped. It couldn't have been a better experience.

Willie actually started crying. There were tears in his eyes. It was a really proud moment for him. I was proud of myself—I made him tear up! And I was proud I now had a skill that could provide meat for my family. When the blood was smeared on my face I felt like a real "buck woman"!

> **"Willie actually started crying. There were tears in his eyes. It was a really proud moment for him."**
> —KORIE

Hunting definitely runs in the family. When our son John Luke first killed a deer we told him how proud we were he was providing for the family.

The first time our daughter Sadie went out hunting, she killed two deer with one shot. There was a doe standing in front of a buck, and she killed them both at the same time with the same shot.

I thought, Well, that's Sadie for you!

That night, I whooped and hollered as I smeared deer blood on Korie's face as a rite of passage.

She says she wasn't looking forward to the blood-smearing part of the experience, but I've seen the video of it, and it looks like she's having a ball. That deer tasted extra good, too, I can swear to that.

It was the greatest hunt of my life—because she was with me and we experienced it together.

Hunting is the taste of freedom.

—Dick Cabela

CHAPTER 10

AMERICA'S HUNTERS IN CHIEF

George Washington, Thomas Jefferson, and Teddy Roosevelt weren't the only American presidents who hunted, not by a long shot.

Lots of folks may not realize many of our greatest presidents, including Abe Lincoln, Franklin Roosevelt, and Dwight Eisenhower, were avid outdoorsmen who would feel right at home in a duck blind or deer stand.

In fact, the White House has been home to a number of duck men, backwoodsmen, amateur gun buffs, and enthusiastic shooters who managed to escape the pressures of being president by sneaking off and hunting in the great outdoors. "Our heroes were hunters, pioneers and Indian fighters," wrote journalist Don Sapatkin. "More than a century after the census declared the American frontier closed, the ethos lives on through popular culture—movie westerns, television, political imagery. Presidents chop wood on the ranch and talk of projecting American power to the other side of the world. It helps if they can knock down a few birds. Few other nations were formed through the violent subjugation of the frontier, and few other nations view hunters—or guns—as we do."

Take Abraham Lincoln, for example. There was a man who knew his way around a gun. He was a back-country boy who grew up on the frontiers of Kentucky and Indiana when they were largely wilderness—an area he described as "a wild region, with many bears and other wild animals still in the woods." The Lincoln family owned two rifles and an old smoothbore musket, weapons they used for self-defense and for shooting the family's dinner. As an adult, Lincoln even wrote a poem, "The Bear Hunt," that recalled the "fun" of a bear chase he witnessed in childhood. Here's part of it:

When first my father settled here,
    'Twas then the frontier line:
The panther's scream, filled night with fear
    And bears preyed on the swine.

But woe for Bruin's short lived fun,
    When rose the squealing cry;
Now man and horse, with dog and gun,
    For vengeance, at him fly. . . .

But leaden death is at his heart,
　Vain all the strength he plies.
And, spouting blood from every part,
　He reels, and sinks, and dies.

And now a dinsome clamor rose,
　'Bout who should have his skin;
Who first draws blood, each hunter knows,
　This prize must always win.

But who did this, and how to trace
　What's true from what's a lie,
Like lawyers, in a murder case
　They stoutly *argufy*.

One day, a young Lincoln spotted a flock of wild turkeys wandering up toward the family's new cabin. He grabbed one of the rifles, shot through a crack in the wall, and killed one of them.

Although the modest Lincoln claimed his hunting skills "never much improved afterwards," he and his buddies hunted turkeys and raccoons regularly. Which, in the words of his kinsman Dennis Hanks, was "pretty much all the time especially so when we got tired of work, which was very often I will assure you." When Lincoln got older, he walked into town and bought a rifle with one of his buddies; they agreed to share it.

For a short time in 1832, during the Black Hawk War, Lincoln served as a captain in the militia. But his men were such a boozy bunch of goofballs that Lincoln was court-martialed and ordered to carry a wooden sword as a humiliating punishment. He was relieved when he was asked to leave military service, but during that time he learned enough about guns to become a gun technology buff. He loved machines and gadgetry, and read *Scientific American* and the *New York Times* to keep up with cutting-edge developments in converting muzzle-loading firearms into breechloaders.

Abraham Lincoln, May 16, 1861
(Library of Congress)

As a wartime president, Lincoln didn't get to do any hunting, but he set up a firing range behind the White House so he could personally test-fire the newest rifle designs for his troops. "Oliver F. Winchester, then head of the Henry Repeating Arms Company, presented Lincoln with an engraved Henry rifle, serial number 6," reported historian Alexander Rose. "Today the Lincoln rifle is one of the crown jewels of the Smithsonian Institution's arms collection."

From 1881 to 1897, the White House was home to three hard-core hunters—Chester Arthur, Benjamin Harrison, and Grover Cleveland. If you check out pictures of these guys, they look like a bunch of sourpusses. I wish I could have seen them hunkered over a campfire, grilling deer meat, trekking across fields, toting shotguns, or blowing duck calls in a blind at sunrise. I bet they had a total blast in the great outdoors!

President Chester Arthur (seated at center) goes hunting,
Yellowstone, 1883 (LIBRARY OF CONGRESS)

The mutton-chopped Chester Arthur was described by the September 11, 1892, issue of the *New York Times* as one of the biggest outdoor sportsmen who had ever been in the White House: "He loved it for every reason—for the fish he caught and the birds he shot, for the pleasure of killing them and the pleasure of eating them, and for the delights of the free life in the camp or the shooting box."

In the summer of 1883, President Arthur took along his friends General Philip Sheridan and Robert Todd Lincoln (son of the late president) on the Northern Pacific Railway to southern Montana for a six-week hunting, camping, and fishing vacation in Yellowstone National Park. Arthur was sick with Bright's disease, which would kill him three years later, but the trip greatly refreshed him. That summer must have been one of the happiest times of his life, far away from the pressures of Washington, DC, riding on horseback in the fresh mountain air, with his fishing rod and breech-loading shotgun.

The five-foot-eleven-inch, two-hundred-fifty-pound Grover Cleveland was a devoted duck man, outdoorsman, fresh- and saltwater fisherman, and wing shooter. He confessed he was "utterly incorrigible and shameless" when it came to his attachment to outdoor sports. He spent days from dawn to dusk in duck blinds along the Chesapeake Bay. The only man to serve two nonconsecutive terms as president—our twenty-second and twenty-fourth—he probably spent more time fishing and hunting than any other president. The press made fun of him for it, but he couldn't have cared less about what he called "petty forms of persecution" that were "nothing more serious than gnat stings suffered on the banks of a stream."

A New Yorker like Chester Arthur, Cleveland was such a big outdoorsman he wrote a book about it, called *Fishing and Shooting Sketches*. He said in his book:

There can be no doubt that certain men are endowed with a sort of inherent and spontaneous instinct which leads them to hunting and fishing indulgence as the most alluring and satisfying of all recreations. I believe, too, that those who thus by instinct and birthright belong to the sporting fraternity and are actuated by a genuine sporting spirit, are neither cruel, nor greedy and wasteful of the game and fish they pursue; and I am convinced that there can be no better conservator the sensible and provident protection of game and fish than those who are enthusiastic in their pursuit, but who, at the same time, are regulated and restrained by the sort of chivalric fairness and generosity, felt and recognized by every true sportsman.

So Cleveland, like Roosevelt, knew that good hunters were true conservationists.

Grover Cleveland; like many other presidents,
he was a duck man (NATIONAL ARCHIVES)

In his White House downtime, Cleveland spent hours curled up with fishing books and magazines, boning up on the habits and traits of different kinds of fish. His favorite outdoor pastime of all was quail shooting. "I am convinced that nothing meets all the requirements of rational, healthful outdoor exercise more completely than quail shooting," he wrote. "It seems to be so compounded of wholesome things that it reaches, with vitalizing effect, every point of mental or physical enervation." Grover Cleveland liked his favorite hunting rifle so much he gave it a nickname—"Death and Destruction."

THE PRESIDENT sandwiched between Cleveland's two terms was Benjamin Harrison. He was another proud duck man and was also the last president to wear a beard, so of course I like him. Not much happened during his one term in the White House, except hunting. He seems to have spent nearly as much time hunting as he did being our nation's leader.

The *New York Times* described President Harrison as "happiest when he is down on the Chesapeake, blasting away at canvasback ducks late in the Fall," and noted, "There is no doubt that his successes with the shotgun afford him keener delight than he experiences from political affairs." Harrison grew up in North Bend, Ohio, where he hunted, fished, chopped wood, and looked after livestock. He became a "gun guy" as an army officer and general during the Civil War. When he became president, he liked to knock off work around noon and spend the rest of the day chasing his grandkids and pets around the White House grounds. He would plan secret hunting trips to the woods of Virginia or Maryland to relax and unwind.

One day in November 1889, Harrison was mighty embarrassed when national newspapers ran the story of how he mistakenly shot a pig owned by a farmer named Gilbert Wooten, having confused it for a raccoon. Another time, he got in trouble for bagging a deer while "night floating" or "jacking"—this meant blinding the deer with a lantern in the front of a drifting boat to ensure a still target. The practice was later banned.

Benjamin Harrison
duck hunting
(NATIONAL ARCHIVES)

But Harrison's greatest hunting legacy was an act of conservation—in 1889 he issued a proclamation that "no person shall kill any otter, mink, marten, sable, or fur seal, or other fur-bearing animal within the limits of Alaska Territory," except as authorized by the secretary of the Treasury, and by doing so he helped regulate and protect an Alaskan seal population that was in danger of being wiped out by commercial overharvesting.

AFTER TEDDY ROOSEVELT, the next hard-core hunter in the Oval Office was Calvin Coolidge, the thirtieth president of the United States, who grew up hunting, trapping, and fishing as a country boy in Vermont. As president he was a fine wing shot and liked to hunt anywhere from South Dakota to Florida, and he especially liked to go hunting with his wife, Grace.

In 1928 the Coolidges went down to Virginia's Blue Ridge Mountains for the Thanksgiving holiday to shoot turkeys, pheasants, and quails. It was a happy trip, but there was one day when nothing seemed to go right for the president. When the weather cleared up on Saturday, December 1, Coolidge, armed with a double shotgun and a $15.50 nonresident hunting license, went quail-hunting on an estate in the Shenandoah Valley near the town of Stuarts Draft.

> **President Coolidge must have looked a little ridiculous in his hunting outfit, which featured a wide Mexican-style sombrero, dress tie, and high-laced boots.**

To tell you the truth, the president must have looked a little ridiculous in his hunting outfit, which featured a wide Mexican-style sombrero, dress tie, and high-laced boots. And he couldn't hit a single bird out of five shots. Maybe the birds were laughing too hard at his hat. Coolidge's hosts complimented him on his rifle-handling skills and apologized for lending him a gun with a barrel so long that maybe his shots couldn't spread out sufficiently. Overall, though, Coolidge had such a good time he couldn't wait for his next hunting trip. Weeks later, he took his wife on a special train from the capital down to Sapelo Island, Georgia, to hunt ring-necked pheasant, wild turkey, and deer.

———————

THE NEXT PRESIDENT who enjoyed hunting was Franklin D. Roosevelt, whose father taught him how to hunt, fish, and ride at the family's vacation home at Campobello, a small island off the coast of Canada. Roosevelt continued a casual enjoyment of hunting and shooting throughout his adulthood. He practiced shooting with the US Marines as secretary of the navy, opossum-hunted with buddies in the woods around his home in Georgia, and worked a Springfield 1903 rifle on the target range. Even after he lost the use of his legs at age thirty-nine, he liked to tag along on opossum hunts by automobile.

As president, FDR gave two great gifts to American hunters and wildlife by building on the legacy of his cousin Teddy Roosevelt. The first was the Civilian Conservation Corps (CCC), a three-million-man civilian environmental army he set up in 1933 to give people work during the Depression and to protect the wilderness, especially American forests, which Roosevelt considered "the lungs of our land [which] purify our air and give fresh strength to our people." The CCC fought forest fires, planted trees, cleared and maintained access roads, reseeded grazing lands, and built wildlife refuges, fish-rearing facilities, water-storage basins, animal shelters, and campgrounds. Roosevelt also expanded America's national forests, national parks, and wildlife refuges by millions of acres.

Franklin Delano Roosevelt, experienced hunter, on the practice range with a Springfield, 1917 (NATIONAL ARCHIVES)

FDR's second great gift was signing the Pittman-Robertson Federal Aid in Wildlife Restoration Act on September 2, 1937, which to this day fosters partnerships between fish and wildlife agencies, the sporting arms industry, conservation groups, and sportsmen and sportswomen to benefit wildlife and to restore, conserve, manage, and enhance wild birds, mammals, and their habitats.

FDR's SUCCESSOR HARRY S. TRUMAN was a Missouri farm boy whose main outdoor sport was power-walking, not hunting, but Roosevelt's top battlefield commander, Dwight D. Eisenhower, known as Ike, was a hard-core, shotgun-packing hunter for much of his adult life.

Eisenhower learned how to hunt and shoot from his childhood hero and mentor in Abilene, Kansas—a legendary trapper, fisher, and guide named Bob Davis. He first met Davis in 1898, when the trapper was in his fifties, so the friendship gave Eisenhower a living link to the days of the Old West. Davis taught young Ike many things, including duck-shooting, field-dressing game, and cooking over a campfire. Together they hunted wolves, raccoons, and quails. As a teenager, Eisenhower's older brother Edgar gave him a sixteen-gauge, pump-action Winchester shotgun, and Ike put it to work hunting wolves, coyotes, and jackrabbits.

Eisenhower remembered spending the happiest days of his life as a young army officer fresh out of West Point. After graduating he was posted to Fort Sam Houston in Texas for a two-year assignment. There he met his future wife, Mamie; usually quit work at midday; and spent much of his free time deer- and dove-hunting, riding, playing poker, drinking beer, and organizing hunting trips across the border into Mexico. Eisenhower was a lifelong fly caster and angler who fished all over America.

Even World War II couldn't stop Eisenhower's passion for hunting. One day in 1942, he took a few hours off to organize a partridge hunt in North Africa. During most of his eight years as president, he shot quails in Georgia every February. "There are three [sports] that I like all for the same reason—golf, fishing, and shooting—and I do because first, they take you into the fields," Eisenhower explained at a presidential press conference on October 15, 1958. "It induces you to take at any one time two or three hours, if you can, when you are thinking of the bird, or that ball or the wily trout. Now, to my mind, it is a very healthy and beneficial kind of thing, and I do it whenever I get a chance," said Eisenhower.

BEFORE DAWN ON THURSDAY, November 17, 1960, two men went deer-hunting in Texas.

What happened next is a mystery.

The first man, John F. Kennedy, had just been elected president. He rarely, if ever, went hunting, though he did occasionally fish, and he was familiar with firearms from his wartime experience as a PT boat skipper and later enjoyed skeet shooting at Camp David.

The second man was Kennedy's vice president–elect, Lyndon Baines Johnson, an enthusiastic deer- and dove-hunter who was hosting JFK as his houseguest at the LBJ Ranch on the Pedernales River near Johnson City, Texas.

Early in the morning, Johnson woke Kennedy up and insisted he come out and kill some deer. "At 6 a.m. they turned out by the ranch house, Johnson in weather beaten cowboy clothes, Kennedy in a checked sports jacket and slacks," wrote historian William Manchester. One observer thought Kennedy, the sophisticated Boston millionaire, looked like he was "on Mars" as he stood in the foothills of Texas, with his hair mussed up and wearing a hunting outfit featuring penny loafers and a white button-down shirt.

There are two versions of what happened next. The first is Kennedy's, which he told to his wife, who in turn told William Manchester. "They left in Johnson's white Cadillac, zooming and jouncing across the fields, and Kennedy was forced to shoot his deer," wrote Manchester. The two deer were pushed into a pasture by Johnson's ranch hands. To Kennedy, Manchester wrote, "shooting tame game was not sport, and he had tried to bow out gracefully," but at Johnson's insistence, he "looked into the face of the life he was about to take," then "fired and quickly turned back to the car."

When Johnson heard in 1966, after he became president, that Manchester's version of the hunt was going to be published in a book about Kennedy's 1963 assassination, he hit the roof. "Forcing that poor man to go hunting?" LBJ hollered to his staff while taping himself on a secret White House recording system. "Hell, he not only killed one deer; he insisted on killing a second! It took three hours and I finally gave up. I said, 'Mr. President, we just can't do it.'"

As for the idea that Kennedy didn't want to shoot the deer: "Poor little deer—he saw it in his eye and he just could not shoot it? Well, hell, he wasn't within 250 yards from it," raged Johnson. "He shot it and he jumped up and hoorahed and put it right on the fender of the car so he could kill another one." LBJ raged sarcastically, "Even if we had made the tragic mistake of forcing this poor man to put up a deer head along with his fish—I do not know who forced him to put up the fish in the Fish Room that he caught on his honeymoon, but I damned sure didn't force him to put up anything. It is just a manufactured lie!"

It goes to show you, and I know this from experience—when

you send two or three hunters into the woods, they can come out with five or ten completely different stories about what happened!

When Lyndon Johnson was president, he often escaped to his Texas ranch, where he kept a specially modified white Lincoln Continental convertible "shooting car" complete with a gun rack and a mobile minibar stocked with his favorite beverages, Cutty Sark and Fresca. He drank, drove, and shot literally at the same time, which is not a combination I'd recommend to anybody!

Lyndon Johnson often escaped to his Texas ranch, where he kept a specially modified white Lincoln Continental convertible "shooting car" complete with a gun rack and a mobile minibar.

"The president carried a chrome-plated 30-30 Winchester rifle in the car, all the time, and he went deer hunting with people, and they hunted from the car," remembered one of Johnson's Secret Service men.

He shot hogs; he shot aoudad sheep. He shot that Winchester a lot. I know, because there were times when we [the Secret Service] ducked under my pickup to keep him from shooting us. If he took people hunting in the convertible, we rode behind in the pickup. He would get on the radio and go, "You blankety-blank Secret Service, you stay back there. I don't want you scaring my deer"—even as he's up in front, going 100 miles an hour. And if that deer started running past his car and came back toward us, we could hear the bullets whizzing over the top, and we'd get under the pickup.

The next big-time hunter in the Oval Office was Jimmy Carter, and he hunted much more responsibly, and safely, than LBJ. "I had a fishing pole in my hands as early as I can remember, and would go hunting with Daddy long before I could have anything to shoot other than a BB gun," Carter wrote of his boyhood near Plains, Georgia, where he hunted deer, duck, and opossum. "I have used weapons since I was big enough to carry one, and now own two handguns, four shotguns and three rifles, two with scopes," Carter wrote in an op-ed to the *New York Times* in 2009. "I use them carefully, for hunting game from our family woods and fields, and occasionally for hunting with my family and friends in other places. We cherish the right to own a gun and some of my hunting companions like to collect rare weapons. One of them is a superb craftsman who makes muzzle-loading rifles, one of which I displayed for four years in my private White House office."

Carter spent a lot of his presidential vacation time hunting or fishing, despite taking a total of only seventy-nine days off—the least of all modern presidents. And, as a rural Southern boy, hunting was in his blood. He once wrote,

Looking back on my hunting days, it seems obvious that the excitement and challenge of hunting was closely related to the acquisition of food. There was never any question about the morality of hunting, but neither was there any acceptance of killing for the sake of a trophy. Landowners, large and small, thought of wild game as one of the important products of the farm, and studied and applied good conservation practices to enhance the value of this harvest in the proper seasons. . . . Even during the Depression years, when many marginal farm families were on the verge of starvation, their prayers of thanksgiving for the land, streams, and woods were devout and sincere.

———

EARLY IN HIS PRESIDENCY, Ronald Reagan went on his first turkey hunt, in Texas, but otherwise his main hunting experience was limited to shooting rattlesnakes at his ranch in California, despite his movie image as an Old West action man. He belonged to a foxhunting club in Los Angeles, but he did more socializing and horseback riding there than foxhunting. Reagan's main outdoor sports were riding horses and chopping wood rather than hunting, but he was a strong friend to the hunting community throughout his life.

———

BILL CLINTON was familiar with guns growing up in Arkansas. "I can still remember the first day when I was a little boy out in the country putting the can on top of a fence post and shooting a .22 at it," he said on the day he signed the Brady Bill in 1993. "I can still remember the first time I pulled a trigger on a .410 shotgun, because I was too little to hold a 12-gauge. This is part of the culture of a big part of America." But truth be told, Clinton was not known as a big hunter. Also, in 1993, the first year of his presidency, Clinton went on a duck-hunting trip, apparently to reassure sportsmen he was a friend to hunters. Wearing camo and waders, he bought a $41 Maryland hunting license, borrowed a twelve-gauge Winchester shotgun, and spent two hours with his buddies lying in wait for mallard ducks at the Fruit Hill Farm hunting lodge on Taylors Island, Maryland. One duck fell, but it was unclear who bagged it.

PRESIDENT GEORGE H. W. BUSH and his son George W. are both natural, hard-core bird hunters who loved to hunt together whenever they could, as well as skeet-shoot on the range at the Camp David presidential retreat. The elder Bush, a World War II fighter pilot, is a lifelong outdoorsman and hunter who learned to hunt as a boy

President George H. W. Bush and his son George W. are both natural, hard-core bird hunters who loved to hunt together.

at his grandparents' lodge in South Carolina, and he loved fish-

George H. W. Bush, hunter (GEORGE BUSH PRESIDENTIAL LIBRARY)

ing as a child in Maine. "The joy of fishing with your son in a river in Wyoming, I'll tell you, it's hard to compete with anything," he once observed. In 1988, when a reporter sternly asked him about a three-day hunting trip, the elder Bush said: "These aren't animals. These are wild quail. You've got to eat." He added: "I don't think I could shoot a deer—quail, that's something else again—tremendously exciting."

I MET PRESIDENT BARACK OBAMA at the 2013 White House Correspondents' Association dinner, where you have to wear a tuxedo, which is not exactly my everyday look. The president was familiar with my TV show, and he was once quoted as saying the Robertson family "seem like a pretty fun bunch."

The next time I saw the president was inside the US Capitol building, where I was a guest of a member of the House of Representatives at the State of the Union address. I was getting ready to get on an elevator when I was told I couldn't just yet because the president was coming.

Before you know it, the president's walking down the hall; he sees me and says, "Willie, what's up?"

So I said to him, "Hey, what's up?" and we had a little polite conversation.

Then the president said, with a big smile, "Where's the tux?" I was impressed he remembered!

"This is my State of the Union attire!" I replied. I think he was teasing me a bit, but I didn't mind.

I don't know if President Obama has ever hunted, but he's said he likes to shoot. "At Camp David, we do skeet shooting all the time," he was quoted as saying in 2014. He also shared some interesting ideas about hunting: "I have a profound respect for the traditions of hunting that trace back in this country for generations. And I think those who dismiss that out of hand make a big mistake." He added, "Part of being able to move this [national gun debate] forward is understanding the reality of guns in urban areas are very different from the realities of guns in rural areas. And if you grew up and your dad gave you a hunting rifle when you were 10, and you went out and spent the

To be honest with you, I'd like to get all our modern presidents out there in the duck blind with some camouflage and a gun, and we could sit out there and talk.

day with him and your uncles, and that became part of your family's traditions, you can see why you'd be pretty protective of that."

To be honest with you, I'd like to get all our modern presidents out there in the duck blind with some camouflage and a gun, and we could sit out there and talk. I'd like to find out what's going on in their brains. I don't shy away from people I disagree with—I want to know why they do what they do and if I can move to change their thinking in some ways. And I'm open myself. I keep an open mind to other people's beliefs.

In a duck blind, it's a fun, perfect time to talk things over. That's the thing about hunting, especially duck-hunting—you can sit out there and talk. It's not like deer-hunting where you've got to be quiet. In between the duck flights you can talk as much as you want.

Believe me, there's been many a friendly Robertson family debate in the duck blind over religion and politics!

———

EVEN THOUGH HE WASN'T A PRESIDENT, there's one hunter who deserves special mention—a big-bearded gentleman named Ernest Hemingway. He was one of the biggest celebrity hunters of his age and one of the greatest writers of the twentieth century.

As a boy he romped through the woods and waters of Michigan, where he learned wing shooting and fly-fishing from his outdoors-loving father. In a fictionalized memoir, he said, "There is much mystic nonsense written about hunting but it is something that is much older than religion. Some are hunters and some are not."

In 1909, the ten-year-old Hemingway was given his own gun by his grandfather in Michigan, and he went on to hunt across the United States and Africa, for antelopes, bears, buffaloes, cheetahs, coyotes, deer, doves, ducks, eagles, elks, guinea fowl, hyenas, impalas, jackals, lions, porcupines, opossums, quails, rabbits, raccoons, sandgrouses, serval cats, sheep, warthogs, and zebras. Before tragically taking his own life in 1961, Hemingway was a highly skilled big-game safari hunter and gun aficionado who had bagged nearly every animal known to man, plus a Pulitzer Prize and a Nobel Prize.

Hemingway was mainly a shotgunner, not a rifleman, though he did enjoy shooting a lightweight 6.5-millimeter Mannlicher-Schoenauer and a custom-made 1930 model .30-06 Griffin & Howe sporting rifle that he simply called a "Springfield," as it was based on the classic 1903 Springfield military rifle platform.

Hemingway's shotguns included the top-of-the-line Winchester Model 21 side-by-side and the sturdy, highly reliable Winchester Model 12 pump-action shotgun, a favorite of a great many hunters. For the biggest game, he used a giant .577 Westley Richards Nitro Express double rifle. For shooting at sharks from his fishing boat, he preferred the gangster-classic, fully automatic Thompson submachine gun.

Hemingway wrote that he considered his Winchester shotgun "from thirty-five years of [their] being together, almost as close a friend and companion with secrets shared and triumphs and disasters not revealed as the other friend a man has all his life."

> **Hemingway considered his Winchester shotgun "almost as close a friend and companion . . . as the other friend a man has all his life."**

He was a crack shot, according to his daughter-in-law Valerie, who witnessed a hair-raising shot fired at Hemingway's sixtieth-birthday party in Spain, attended by his wife, Mary, and the world's greatest matador, Antonio Ordóñez: "Mary rented a shooting gallery from a traveling carnival, and it became the main attraction when Ernest, to the horror and fascination of the onlookers, blasted the ash from Antonio's lighted cigarette with a .22 rifle as the matador held the butt between his lips." Don't try that at home, folks.

Hemingway's hunting tales, which he told in stories like *A Farewell to Arms*, *The Green Hills of Africa*, "The Short Happy Life of Francis Macomber," "The Snows of Kilimanjaro," and *True at First Light*, and in many articles he wrote for magazines like *Esquire*, *Vogue*, and *Look*, helped bring the adventure, danger, and romance of hunting to millions of Americans.

I breathe because my body needs oxygen.
I eat because my body must have energy.
I hunt because I am a hunter.
These are simple things which I accept,
and perhaps no explanation is possible.
—Charley Dickey, *Opening Shots and Parting Lines*

CHAPTER 11

AMERICAN HUNTING TODAY

Every day across the country, thousands of American hunters like me do something we rarely talk about: We give our meat away. A lot of it. We give it to people who need it, to families who are hungry. Hunters don't do it for publicity or to pat themselves on the back. They do it because it's the right thing to do and a great way to help our fellow man.

In the Robertson family, when we were growing up we used to take our ducks and go to certain neighborhoods and drop them off with needy people. These folks were in no condition to go out hunting in the freezing cold, but they sure appreciated having the free meat.

In fact, just a few weeks ago, I hunted on a friend's property, and he has a program with his church where he takes the deer to the processor and it gets all processed into steaks and ground meat and into packages. He's got two big freezers in his church, and people from the church will just take what they need if they need some meat. It's free and we provide it.

I've participated in a great program called Hunters for the Hungry. You can take your deer and donate it and they process it and distribute it to people who need food. If you don't have enough freezer space to handle all the deer you kill, this way you can donate it to someone in your community who needs food. Throughout mankind's history, when a group went out to hunt, they'd bring back food to feed the people of the village. It still happens today. Just imagine how many people you could feed with the stuff you shoot and bring in, the more organized you get.

If you don't have enough freezer space to handle all the deer you kill, Hunters for the Hungry is a way you can donate it to someone in your community who needs food.

For the past twenty-five years, a quiet, powerful campaign of love and compassion has grown across US hunting communities in over twenty states. It goes by many names, like Hunters for the Hungry, Farmers and Hunters Feeding the Hungry, Donate Your Deer, and Sportsmen Against Hunger. They are team efforts between committed hunters, sportsmen's groups, faith-based organizations, meat processors, state meat inspectors, and hunger relief organizations to reach out and help feed hungry families, free of charge.

Here's how a typical program works. A hunter drops off a field-dressed whitetail deer at a participating butcher or meat-processing facility. The meat is processed, cut, ground, packaged, and frozen, sometimes for a small fee, and distributed to homeless shelters, soup kitchens, and food banks, so hungry families, children, and elderly people can enjoy highly nutritious food. State game wardens pitch in, too—by donating animals seized as evidence from poachers. Ranches help out also, by culling deer when their herds get overpopulated and donating the harvested deer.

A single deer can yield about thirty to thirty-five pounds of processed meat, or an average of one hundred sixty meals. That's one of the reasons I love deer hunting—you can eat a lot more food off a deer than you can a duck!

In Tennessee, where such programs have provided over three million meals to needy people across the state, Marcia Wells of the Mid-South Food Bank explained, "We get ground meat and roasts in beautifully packaged 1- to 2-pound portions. We're always looking for more high-protein products, and venison is a great one. We're just thrilled to have it." Local meat processor Stu Burris, who participates in the program, explained that you can use venison for everything—tacos, soup, chili, stew, spaghetti, meatloaf, anything you'd use regular store-bought beef for. "I always tell my hunters to take care of their own families first, but then once their freezers are full, I tell them there's just no way you can go wrong by donating a deer to a program like Hunters for the Hungry. It's a win-win any way you slice it."

In Maine, Jason Hall, the director of the Department of Agriculture, Conservation, and Forestry's Emergency Food Assistance Program, called the state's nearly twenty-year-old Hunters for the Hungry program one of Maine's best-kept secrets, with about 5,000 pounds of deer, moose, and bear meat being donated every year by hunters and wardens to the help feed the hungry to 246 food pantries, soup kitchens, and shelters across the state. "We're a hunter's paradise," said Hall. "We have a lot of generous people. The wild game is a high-protein, low-fat source of food. It does

American hunter in Maine, 1886 (LIBRARY OF CONGRESS)

make a big difference in Maine." One hunter from Maine by the name of Grant Owens said, "My family and I firmly believe it's our social responsibility to contribute," adding, "Venison is very high in protein and it's very lean, so it's the perfect thing to give to families in need who are typically protein deficient."

In Texas, which is a state that has both a huge population of deer and, unfortunately, a growing number of people in need of food assistance, the Hunters for the Hungry campaign and Donate Your Deer program have in recent years provided ten thousand pounds of food a year. "We have always been game for game," said Eric Cooper, the president and CEO of the San Antonio Food Bank. "It's pretty lean and a great source of protein." Mike Leggett, a Texas hunter, explained, "I've been donating venison to Hunters for the Hungry for most of the 20 years the program has been in effect, probably more than 100 animals altogether. That doesn't make me a great humanitarian, just one of countless hunters in states all over the country who recognize a worthwhile program."

So far, across America, nearly 250 million meals have been donated by hunters to the hungry.

I hope you and I can help the campaign grow by leaps and bounds.

———

HUNTING IS THRIVING across America—and many wildlife populations are booming.

Many folks may not realize it, but there is a direct connection between the two. There are nearly fourteen million hunters in America, and the number is growing as new hunters join the ranks, including women and younger folks. In the last five years measured by the US Fish and Wildlife Service, the number of hunters in America increased by 9 percent. Hundreds of millions of dollars generated in hunting taxes, licenses, and fees go directly to support federal and state wildlife and habitat conservation programs. About 680,000 jobs in America are supported by hunting.

"Over the last 75 years, hunters and recreational shooters have shown their willingness to pay a little extra for their excise-taxable gear, knowing that their purchases would directly support conservation along with a multitude of wildlife-related activities," said Jeff Vonk, secretary of the South Dakota Department of Fish, Game and Parks and president of the Association of Fish and Wildlife Agencies. "The financial contributions of sportsmen and women help state fish and wildlife agencies restore and manage wildlife and their habitats; open and maintain access for all, including shooting ranges; and they keep the public safe by supporting hunter education."

Thanks to the work, passion, and money of countless hunters and nonhunters alike, many species that were once thought on the verge of extinction have been transformed through conservation and responsible practices into healthy and well-managed populations.

By the 1920s, the whitetail deer population in America had plunged to about three hundred thousand. Now there are well over twenty million. Wild turkey numbered less than thirty thousand then; now there are over four million, in every state but Alaska. The pronghorn antelope population had collapsed to just twenty-five thousand and North American elk to fifty thousand, and now there are more than a million antelopes and elks. Then, wood ducks were almost extinct; now there are over three million. Then, there were around five hundred bison; now there are three hundred fifty thousand.

Wood duck poised for takeoff, Oregon (GEORGE GENTRY, US FISH & WILDLIFE SERVICE)

The heroes who helped pull off this conservation miracle include many legendary American hunters, and people who were drawn to the wilderness by hunting and fishing.

Hunters helped create, push for, and implement conservation measures for one reason—it's the right thing to do.

———

As a hunter, you've always got new things to learn; there are new animals and weapons to study, and new adventures to look forward to.

I love my work, but between running a company and doing a television show and all of the things I do, I actually don't get to hunt as much as I'd like to!

I only recently started turkey-hunting, over in Florida, which was loads of fun. I hunted bears for the first time this year in New Jersey, with buckshot and a twelve-gauge shotgun. I didn't get any bears, but it was interesting. It was about nine degrees out there in the woods. My friends and I were sitting out there in the daylight, huddled around a campfire, freezing our butts off, and eating a box of doughnuts. C'mon, who doesn't love doughnuts? Bears love them too, and the delicious smell drew one toward us.

We heard a heavy *crunch, crunch* on the snow not far off, and we slowly and quietly grabbed our guns, scanning the trees for our prey. We couldn't see the bear, but it felt no more than a hundred yards away.

BOOM! A blast came out of nowhere, followed by a thud on the snow.

Somebody else shot him. I never realized how many hunters there are in New Jersey, but there sure was a bunch on that mountain.

I'm going back there next spring—I've already got my next New Jersey bear hunt set up.

Last season I got in twenty-three days of deer-hunting in November and December. You think about hunting seasons in the

The hunt begins (Copyright © Buck Commander)

winter, Christmas, November—that's when our business is really hot and heavy. We're hunting and we're selling; that's when everyone's buying products.

There's lots of hunting I haven't done yet, that I dream of doing.

I'd love to go to hunting in Alaska someday. I've never been there. I haven't done a lot of elk-hunting, but I would love to. Hopefully next year I'll be able to get out west and bag some elks. I haven't done much hunting in higher elevations, especially with archery, where you have to get up close to a 1,500-pound animal and really get in their face.

The hunting seasons open up earlier the farther north you go. You could probably go five or six months traveling down from Canada, hunting all the way. I'd love to take a few months off and just follow down the seasons!

When we were little, a big pot of squirrels and gravy was one of my favorite things to eat. My father is a great squirrel hunter. When it comes to squirrel-hunting season, I'm not as hard-core as Phil, who typically will go out and hunt squirrel in his socks so he doesn't make much noise. He'll slip around the woods in his socks with a .22. It's a little bullet, so it's all or nothing with that.

> **I'm not as hard-core as Phil, who typically will go out and hunt squirrel in his socks so he doesn't make much noise.**

The squirrels in our yard were always off-limits, though—our mom, Miss Kay, was familiar with them and she banned hunting them!

While I've been out deer-hunting, I've also hunted a lot of wild hogs. They're very overpopulated and a big nuisance. They'll come in and eat everything and tear up the yard. Typically, the local landowners would love you to kill a couple of hogs if you see them. The trick is getting them without messing up your deer hunt as well! There's been many a hunt where we've been successful with the deer, and I've also gotten a hog as well.

We never had a real "hog problem" on our property. We were lucky that way. That is, until one day when Phil looked up and saw a gang of six mean-looking hogs marching through our woods. He thought, *Well, they're finally here!* We didn't want the hogs tearing up all our crops, so Phil proceeded to shoot all six of them, and we took them back to give them to a friend. We were going to help him clean them and eat them.

Well, you'll never guess what happened. Our friend was cleaning those hog carcasses with us, and lo and behold this guy looks up and says, "Hey, I've got six pet hogs that I raised, and they got out and I'm looking for them. Has anyone seen them?" He looked over at me, but by then they'd already been cleaned, skinned, and prepared to be eaten by us. His eyes got bigger as the truth dawned on him.

"We thought they were wild," I said sheepishly, and we gave him back his hogs.

He wasn't really raising the hogs as pets; he was raising them to eat. He got his meat back, but I think he was a little sad.

———————

WITH OUR TV SHOWS, I hope we've brought some good positive awareness to hunting. I like to focus on the social aspect of hunting, the fun nature of the hunting experience, not just the technicalities of hunting—the deer camp, the duck blind, the friends, the family, the campfire, the dinner table, the vacation feeling, all the fun stuff that happens in camp.

We celebrate family values. We're positive, God-fearing, gun-toting people. And we're funny. Funny helps. I think viewers sense the authenticity of us as people. Our show is clean, too; you can watch it as a family. Kids and grandparents can watch together. If it's appealing and everyone can sit down and watch, then it is a unique kind of show nowadays.

We're positive, God-fearing, gun-toting people. And we're funny. Funny helps.

I think even nonhunters see us as entertaining, and hopefully we show people who hunt and outdoorsmen as positive people anyone can relate to. The program shows that we're successful at our business, and people respect that no matter where they live. And they see us praying together, having meals together as a family, and spending time together. Whether they are urban or country, I think a lot of folks like that.

———

I'M A BIG RIFLE GUY, 'cause I do a lot of deer-hunting. What's my favorite? I'd say my Savage seven-millimeter magnum with an accu-trigger. I actually built mine. I went to the company manufacturing facility and built it myself. Those Savages, man, I'll tell you what: They say on the box they're the most accurate rifles there are. And it's true.

When you think about it, the history of hunting weapons in America has been amazing. Over the last two centuries, the flintlocks and muzzle-loading rifles gave way to breechloaders, metallic cartridges, repeaters, telescopic sights, and space-age designs and materials. In the shotgun world, breech loading, cartridge ammo, and choke boring were all developed by 1887, and when the magazine repeater Winchester Model 1897 pump shotgun came out, it ushered in the age of pumps and autoloaders.

Some classic weapon designs endure for decades, like the rugged, reliable German-designed Mauser Model 98 bolt-action center-fire rifle and its clone, the US-government-produced 1903 Springfield service rifle chambered for the .30-06 cartridge, which was so close to the Mauser that a court made Uncle Sam pay royalties. The bolt-action Winchester Model 70 rifle, which has been going strong for nearly eighty years, is a favorite of big-game hunters. The Model 94 Savage/Stevens single-barrel shotgun has put food on family dinner tables for a century and inspired many young people to hunt. Nineteen fifty-five was a big year for hunting technology, as it marked the dawn of the big-game-hunting handgun, when Smith & Wesson and Ruger chambered a long-barreled revolver for a big, very powerful cartridge—the .44 Remington Magnum. In 1887, the J. Stevens Arms & Tool Company came out with the .22 long rifle rimfire, one of the most popular handgun and rifle cartridges ever, and today it remains an essential weapon platform for competition shooting and hunting squirrel, deer, and small game.

I've always enjoyed hunting with different kinds of weapons: rifle, shotgun, bow, and crossbow. I follow the season. If it's bow season, I'll use a bow. If I can use a crossbow, I will. I also love having a little extra distance—compared to a bow—and more confidence in my shot. I'm not trying to prove anything to anybody. Crossbows are safe and fun. You can practice in your backyard.

I'm glad that Louisiana opened up the archery season to crossbows in 2008. I shoot the new Buck Commander Xtreme by Barnett Crossbows. It's light, and I love the handle on the forend. It's much easier to use when you're tree-stand hunting. I was probably the first person to shoot a deer with it, back in December 2014. I took a 180-inch Louisiana buck with that crossbow. It was awesome.

Willie Robertson bow hunting (COPYRIGHT © BUCK COMMANDER)

I got into bow hunting because I had friends who did it. Bow season typically starts a month or so earlier than any other weapons season, so you can go out early. The nice thing about bow hunting is you can practice year-round, pretty much anywhere you have a small yard, as long as you've got thirty yards where you can shoot. You can't do that with guns. Trying to hit targets gives you a peaceful feeling of concentration, and it becomes a hobby in and of itself.

227

What attracted me to bow hunting was how close you can get to the deer, say forty yards or so. It's a whole different ball game—you can hear him breathing, hear him eating an acorn; it's quite a rush.

When I draw back on a bow or crossbow, I feel like I'm connecting with hunters, warriors, and sportsmen going back thousands of years, like Robin Hood, the Japanese samurai, the great Inuit and Native American hunters, and the Olympic archers of today. I can imagine stalking and killing Alaskan brown bear, Rocky Mountain grizzly, Quebec caribou with giant antlers, moose, and elk with five-foot racks or a bobcat or wolverine.

I also feel connected to American bow-hunting pioneers like Will and Maurice Thompson, and Saxton Pope and Art Young, who helped make the sport popular in the early twentieth century

Willie Robertson, taking aim (COPYRIGHT © BUCK COMMANDER)

through books, lectures, and films. When Pope was in medical school at the University of California, he met Ishi, the last member of the Yahi tribe, who taught Pope and his friend Young the art of traditional bow hunting. These three men in turn inspired American bow-hunting legends like Fred Bear, Larry Koller, Howard Hill, Melvin Johnson, the Wensel brothers, and Chuck Adams, perhaps the greatest bow hunter in the world today.

As Fred Bear once said, "The history of the bow and arrow is the history of mankind."

———

ONE OF THE MOST INTERESTING hunting stories I've heard recently is about Mark Zuckerberg, the founder and CEO of Facebook.

One day a few years ago, Zuckerberg had a pig roast at his house. Some of his friends told him they loved eating pork, but they didn't want to think about the fact the pig was once a living creature. "That just seemed irresponsible to me," Zuckerberg explained in an e-mail that was published by *Fortune* magazine. "I don't have an issue with anything people choose to eat, but I do think they should take responsibility and be thankful for

"Many people forget that a living being has to die for you to eat meat, so my goal revolves around not letting myself forget that and being thankful for what I have."
—MARK ZUCKERBERG

what they eat rather than trying to ignore where it came from."

So in 2011, Zuckerberg decided to do something I really admire—he decided to eat meat only from animals he killed himself for a year. "This year, my personal challenge is around being thankful for the food I have to eat," he explained. "I think many people forget that a living being has to die for you to eat meat, so my goal revolves around not letting myself forget that and being thankful for what I have." He spent this time mostly eating vegetarian, but in May of that year he announced on his Facebook page, "I just killed a pig and a goat." Silicon Valley chef Jesse Cool, who introduced Zuckerberg to local farmers and advised him on killing his first pig, chicken, and goat, explained, "He cut the throat of the goat with a knife, which is the most kind way to do it." Zuckerberg's first kill was a lobster that he boiled alive. "The most interesting thing was how special it felt to eat it after having not eaten any seafood or meat in a while," Zuckerberg reported.

Zuckerberg also followed a practice that many Native American hunters did—he decided "to thank the animals whose lives [he took] in order to eat them," as a way of reminding himself to be thankful. On September 27, 2011, *Fortune* magazine editor Patricia Sellers explained, "Zuckerberg has learned to hunt, according to people close to him. He got a hunting license and recently shot and killed a bison."

I think Zuckerberg's yearlong challenge was a great example to all of us, and an honest and honorable way to honor nature—and himself.

CHAPTER 12

VOICES FROM THE HEART OF AMERICAN HUNTING

I'm not the only one who loves hunting and sees the benefits of it—whether personal, to bring our families closer together, or to help others. Below are quotes from some other hunters who also love the hunt and the great outdoors.

Hunting is not merely taking an animal's life, but it is the preparation, the stalk, the matching of skill and patience with creatures so in tune with their environment they almost always know you are there before they see you. It is the peace and joy of nature and being an honest part of creation even if just for a moment. I think women innately crave this and once exposed often embrace it.

All of my hunting has been filled with happy memories.

I was especially blessed to enjoy many days in the field with my dearest husband. There is a unique joy of spending the night in front of a campfire retelling the day's adventure with a loved one and I would never trade any of those nights with my family. When we introduced our children to hunting, it allowed us to share something intimate about ourselves with them in a way we could never explain otherwise. They got to feel the same mixture of emotions we did. They got to experience the beauty of God's creation the way He created it. When they began to introduce their loved ones, it made me realize that my grandchildren and great-grandchildren will understand that same part of me not because anyone told them, but because they experienced it. We create these memories. They become a part of us. And they bond us together eternally.

I have great hope for the future of American hunting. American hunters are the greatest conservationists the world has ever seen and when we pass on our traditions and our love for the outdoors, our children begin to understand the importance of wild places. Hunting gives them an honest relationship with the outdoors. It teaches them humility and patience and perseverance. It teaches them the kinds of things they will never learn watching nature videos or visiting zoos. While those things are great, they lack the intimacy and satisfaction of a long day of hunting. And it is that intimacy that compels them to pass on the traditions and opportunities to future generations. As humans, we crave adventure—real adventure. And that means stepping away from the well-worn path sometimes. As long as we make time to introduce others to the beauty of hunting, it will continue to be a treasured pastime for generations to come.

There is a reason hunters spend so much time, energy, and money on conservation causes. They donate to so many dedicated conservation groups. They volunteer for those same groups. And any hunter fortunate enough to own land often spends hours and hours enhancing and preserving the natural habitat to ensure that the animals they love to pursue not only survive, but thrive. In my view, conservation and recreational hunting are inseparable. Recreational hunting—the kind most practiced today—is more about the experience than the kill. In order to have that unique and wholesome experience wild places must exist. Hunters, if allowed to pursue their passions, will forever ensure those places and those animals they love remain. These places are a gift from God and God's gifts are meant to be passed on to another.

—Mary Cabela, hunter and cofounder of Cabela's

If most hunters are like me, they began hunting because they were introduced to it at some point—most often from a parent to a child. From there it becomes so much more than heading to the woods or field to shoot game. It becomes, at its core, a relationship builder. It enhances relationships with the people we share the field with and it enhances our relationships with the outdoors and the animals we pursue. I believe you become far more connected to the beauty and sometimes brutality of the natural world when you spend time hunting and fishing. We often do not consider the long and storied history of the American hunting culture and why it is something that has been easily and passionately passed on from generation to generation. We simply remember how much we enjoyed spending time outdoors with our loved ones and we wish to pass that joy on to others.

—David Cabela, outdoor writer

Hunting combines an inherent passion for the outdoors, fascination with nature and desire for adventure that extends the borders of one's current limits. Realization of hunting's impact on one's spirit can only be achieved through shared experiences in a brotherhood bound by mutual passion for the grand theater of the outdoors.

—Mark Morgan, author, *A View from Blind and Field*

Through hunting, we test our bodies, wits and hearts in the natural world, and we sharpen our stamina, courage and prowess. We become keenly aware of the elements, the animal tracks in the mud or sand, our own heartbeat and the barely audible whispers of guide and companions. We feel alive.

—Jay Ann Cox, hunter

It has always seemed to me that any man is a better man for being a hunter. This sport confers a certain constant alertness, and develops a certain ruggedness of character. . . . Moreover, it allies us to the pioneer past. In a deep sense, this great land of ours was won for us by hunters.

—Archibald Rutledge, educator, author, and poet

If you have learned nothing else from hunting, you have learned patience and stubbornness and concentration on what you really want at the expense of what there is to shoot. You have learned that man can as easily be debased as ennobled by a sport, and that optimism is the vital ingredient of any sort of chase, from girls to greater kudu.

If the sentimentalist were right, hunting would develop in men a cruelty of character. But I have found that it inculcates patience, demands discipline and iron nerve, and develops a serenity of spirit that makes for long life and long love of life.

—Archibald Rutledge, educator, author, and poet

Hunting is one of those pleasures that you won't understand if you have to have it explained, which is good because folks who enjoy it can't fully explain why.

—Ron Spomer, outdoor writer and photographer

The essence of being a really good hunter is, paradoxically, to love the particular species of game you're after and have enormous respect and consideration for it.

—Hugh Fosburgh, author

Modern man desperately needs to get in touch with the tides, with the wind and the rain, with the forests and streams and mountains and their changeless and sustaining rhythms, and hunting or fishing is one way this is achieved.

—Nelson Bryant, outdoor columnist, *New York Times*

Animals have consciousness and spirit as do humans; and hunting them respectfully for food grounds us in the cycles of nature from which modern culture is increasingly divorced.

—Ted Kerasote, author

The thrill in caribou hunting is not the shooting or the challenge of the stalk, for when caribou appear, the harvesting is easy. Instead, it is the sight of these splendid beasts flooding across unspoiled wilderness. And it is the opportunity to thrust oneself briefly into a hunting culture and join in an ancient pursuit that brings hunters back again and again.

—Jerome B. Robinson, caribou hunter

We are the biggest conservationists in the world as hunters. We raise money, we buy tags and licenses, and all that money goes toward wildlife management and habitat management, and on top of that, which I think is why more women are getting involved, it's organic wild game; you don't have to get pesticide, hormone beef from the supermarket—you know where its coming from. And that's a huge thing.

—Eva Shockey, hunter

A sportsman may have hunted deer, turkey, elk and bears for years with the greatest of success; but until he has taken his sheep, until he has matched his brains, his endurance and his skills with those inhabitants of the rocky peaks, he is still but a sophomore.

—Jack O'Connor, outdoor writer

To most of us, hunting—and in particular, deer hunting—is a way to break away from our daily lives and to get out into the woods, matching wits with an extremely wary quarry. Whether we succeed or fail in our hunt depends not so much on luck but on our preparation, our skill.

—Jay Cassell, author

If hunting is an ancient, obsolete, and outmoded way to live, then I will lie down on the blessed earth, let the wet moss saturate my body, open my eyes to the heaven beyond these boughs, and shout aloud my gratitude for the gift of birth in a time before hunting vanishes from the realm of human experience.

—Richard K. Nelson, author

If someone who has never owned a gun or a rod should ask me what I have gotten out of nearly fifty years of fishing and hunting, the very nature of the question would prompt me to say, "Nothing." It would be practically impossible to explain to such a person what the practice of these sports in boyhood means to a man later in life. He could never even guess that sitting by a pond, waiting for a bite, or watching a woodchuck hole could lay the foundation for patience and perseverance; that a full creel of the legal limit of birds developed restraint, nor would he see that endless smiles in pure air and bright sunshine meant health and strength for better manhood.

—Austin D. Haight, author

The old man used to say that the best part of hunting and fishing was the thinking about going and the talking about it after you got back.

The best thing about hunting and fishing is that you

don't have to actually do it to enjoy it. You can go to bed every night thinking how much fun you had twenty years ago, and it all comes back as clear as moonlight.

—Robert Ruark, outdoor writer

When I was young, I was a hunter, walking wooded hillsides with confident steps and a gun in my hand. I knew the blur of wings, the rocketing form, and the Great Moment that only hunters know, when all existence draws down to two points and a single line. And the universe holds its breath. And what may be and what will be meet and become one— before the echo returns to its source.

—Pete Dunne, birding writer

While hunting, I've cried at the beauty of mountains covered in snow. I've learned to own up to my past mistakes, to admit them freely, and then to behave better the next time around. I've learned to see the earth as a thing that breathes and writhes and brings forth life. I see these revelations as a form of grace and art, as beautiful as the things we humans attempt to capture through music, dance, and poetry.

—Steven Rinella, outdoorsman and author

Life in the open is one of my finest rewards. I enjoy and become completely immersed in the high challenge and increased opportunity to become for a time, a part of nature. Deer hunting is a classical exercise in freedom. It is a return to fundamentals that I instinctively feel are basic and right.

—Fred Bear, founding father of modern bow hunting

Others around me may opt to eat only plants, nuts and fruits. Still others may employ faceless strangers to procure their meats, their leather, their feathers, and all those niceties and necessities of life. Such is their right, of course, and I wish them well. All I ask in return is no one begrudge me—and all of us who may answer the primordial stirrings within our hunter's souls—my right to do some of these things myself.

—M. R. James, hunter

There are those who say the kill doesn't matter. They are fools or liars. I can laugh at misses, pass up an easy shot when there is a reason, and come home skunked but happy. All of that doesn't matter. The kill matters. And the manner of the kill matters.

—Robert Elman, outdoor writer

I did not mind killing anything, any animal, if I killed it cleanly, they all had to die and my interference with the nightly and the seasonal killing that went on all the time was very minute and I had no guilty feeling at all. We ate the meat and kept the hides and horns.

—Ernest Hemingway, writer

A particular virtue of wildlife ethics is that the hunter ordinarily has no gallery to applaud or disapprove of his acts, they are dictated by his own conscience, rather than a mob of onlookers. It is difficult to exaggerate the importance of this fact.

—Aldo Leopold, founding father of modern wildlife

management

I do not hunt for the joy of killing but for the joy of living, and the inexpressible pleasure of mingling my life, however briefly, with that of a wild creature that I respect, admire and value.

—John Madson, naturalist and conservationist

Some people ask why men go hunting. They must be the kind of people who seldom get far from highways. What do they know of the tryst a hunting man keeps with the wind and the trees and the sky? Hunting? The means are greater than the end, and every . . . hunter knows it.

—Gordon MacQuarrie, outdoor writer

The number one rule in duck hunting is to go where the ducks are.

—Jase Robertson, American hunter

Since I was a little kid, I've had this profound connection and love for the deep, dark, unmolested woods. I've always had a longing to be in the deep woods or in the water. I want to be on lakes, streams, and rivers and surrounded by everything that comes with it—the ducks, birds, fish, and other wildlife. I guess it's in my DNA, and I just love being out there. Even to this day, it's where I want to be.

—Phil Robertson, American hunter

———

FOR THE ROBERTSON FAMILY, I reckon that hunting will be a part of our lives for many years to come. It gives us spiritual fulfillment, family bonding, and physical sustenance. It is, in large part, our life.

My oldest son, John Luke, loves to hunt, and my daughter Sadie loves to hunt when she has the time. My two youngest are not big into hunting yet but we'll see if they get involved or not. They certainly are getting involved in the business.

When one of my children kills a deer, we take it home and clean it and eat it. As a family, we like to share our successes—if one of us got one, we all got one. It's a collective feeling. We say a

Willie Robertson and John Luke
(COPYRIGHT © WILLIE ROBERTSON)

prayer of thanks for the fact that John Luke or Sadie provided supper for us that night. That meat will feed my family for a long time.

It's a great time to be an American hunter.

Though some folks may not appreciate our history, we know we have a lot to be proud of.

We have a rich heritage to uphold. We have done great things for Earth, for wildlife, and for our fellow man.

And we have great responsibilities to carry forward, to hunt responsibly, safely, and ethically, and to share our bounty with those less fortunate than we are.

As we hunt in the fields of the Lord, let us always keep in mind the instruction He gave us in Genesis: "Be fruitful, and multiply, and replenish the earth."

Willie Robertson, American Hunter
(COPYRIGHT © WILLIE ROBERTSON)

SOURCE NOTES

CHAPTER 1: AN AMERICAN HUNTER IN THE FIELDS OF THE LORD

"The hunter crouches in his blind": Ogden Nash, "The Hunter," in Mary Ellen Chase, *Values in Literature* (Houghton Mifflin, 1965), 285.

"Hunting is our heritage, it is our poetry": "The Role and Value of Hunting," Conservation Force, https://www.conservationforce.org/rolehorn .html.

"If more fathers were woodsmen": Archibald Hamilton Rutledge, *An American Hunter* (Frederick A. Stokes, 1937), 141.

"who know well the game they hunt": Conservation Force, "The Role and Value of Hunting."

CHAPTER 2: A HUNTER'S PARADISE

"It is the feminine": Marsha Bol, *North, South, East, West: American Indians and the Natural World* (Carnegie Museum of Natural History, 1998), 100.

"Everything the Kiowa had came from the buffalo": Steve Sheinkin and Tim Robinson, *Which Way to the Wild West?* (Macmillan, 2010), 173.

"it was hard to say where the animal ended": Valerius Geist, *Buffalo Nation* (Voyageur Press, 1996), 37. Sources for background on early American hunters include George Laycock, *The Hunters and the Hunted* (Outdoor Life Books, 1990), and *The Story of American Hunting and Firearms* (McGraw Hill, 1959).

"The scene that we now beheld": George Bird Grinnell, *Pawnee Hero Stories and Folk-tales: With Notes on the Origin, Customs, and Character of the Pawnee People* (Forest and Stream, 1889), 270–302.

"Father, you are the Ruler": Ibid.

"Side by side, at the head of the column": Ibid.

CHAPTER 3: THE LONG HUNTERS

"From a flat bar of soft iron": John Dillin, *The Kentucky Rifle* (George Shumway, 1967), xi.

"Each backwoodsman was not only a small farmer"; "He lived out in the woods": Theodore Roosevelt, *The Winning of the West, Vol. 1: The Backwoodsmen* (Putnam, 1889), 114 and 123.

"second paradise"; "the Garden of God": Daniel Boone, statement to Kentucky legislature, January 18, 1812, printed in *Weekly Register*, March 13, 1813.

"We found everywhere abundance of wild beasts": Cecil Hartley, *The Life and Times of Colonel Daniel Boone* (Perkins, 1902), 359.

"you may be sure the wasps and yellow-jackets": John Bakeless, *Daniel Boone: Master of the Wilderness* (University of Nebraska Press, 1939), 52.

"I had gained the summit of a commanding ridge": Daniel Boone, "Adventures of Col. D. Boone," *Scots Magazine*, January 1791, 8.

"On the 16th of June, before sunrise": Wilbur Fisk Gordy, *American*

Leaders and Heroes: A Preliminary Text-book in United States History (Scribner's, 1903), 231.

"My footsteps have often been marked with blood": John Filson and Daniel Boone, *The Discovery, Settlement, and Present State of Kentucky* (Stockdale, 1793), 48.

CHAPTER 4: THE FOUNDING HUNTERS

"the best horseman of his age": John Foley, ed., *The Jeffersonian Cyclopedia* (Funk & Wagnalls, 1900), 928.

"Went fox hunting with the gentlemen": Letter from R. A. Austen Leigh, *Virginia Magazine of History and Biography*, July 1905, 210–11.

"After an early breakfast": Alexander Henry Higginson, *Two Centuries of Foxhunting* (Collins, 1946), 29.

"Went a ducking between breakfast": Ibid., 33.

"The situation is a heavenly one": "Visit to Washington," *West Virginia Historical Magazine Quarterly*, January 1901, 63.

"No person whatever shall hunt upon my grounds": James Hosmer Penniman, *George Washington at Mount Vernon on the Potomac* (Mount Vernon Ladies Association of the Union, 1921), 38.

"Very good, sir": George Washington Parke Custis and Mary Randolph Custis Lee, *Memoirs of Washington* (Englewood Publishing, 1859), 452.

"[Jefferson] was a keen hunter": James Parton, "College Days of Thomas Jefferson," *Atlantic Monthly*, January 1872, 25.

"I advise the gun": Jefferson to Peter Carr, August 19, 1785, Monticello .org, "Firearms," the Thomas Jefferson Encyclopedia, http://www .monticello.org/site/research-and-collections/firearms.

"squirrels and partridges": Isaac Jefferson, *Memoirs of a Monticello Slave*, Monticello.org, "Hunting," the Thomas Jefferson Encyclopedia, http://www.monticello.org/site/research-and-collections/hunting.

"A fine morning": Reuben Gold Thwaites, *Original Journals of the Lewis & Clark Expedition* (Dodd, Mead, 1904), 369, 370.

"1 Pair Pocket Pistols": National Firearms Museum online exhibit, "U.S. Harpers Ferry Model 1792 Flintlock Rifle," http://www.nramuseum .org/guns/the-galleries/a-prospering-new-republic-1780-to-1860 /case-8-romance-of-the-long-rifle/us-harpers-ferry-model-1792 -flintlock-rifle-repro.aspx.

"After the council was over, we shot the air gun": Ibid., 211.

"In the evening we saw a Brown or Grisley beare": Paul Schullery, *Lewis and Clark Among the Grizzlies: Legend and Legacy in the American West* (Globe Pequot, 2002), 45.

"Capt. Clark and Drewyer killed the largest": Thomas Schmidt, *Journals of Lewis and Clark* (National Geographic Society, 2003), 146.

CHAPTER 5: THE AGE OF THE MOUNTAIN MEN

Details of Colter's Run: Burton Harris, *John Colter: His Years in the Rockies* (University of Nebraska Press, 1993), 123–34.

"I wanted to be the first to view a country": Robert M. Utley, *After Lewis and Clark: Mountain Men and the Paths to the Pacific* (University of Nebraska Press, 2004), 90.

"I put my needle sticking": Alton Pryor, *California's Hidden Gold: Nuggets from the State's Rich History* (Stagecoach, 2002), 23.

"I started into the mountains": Edwin Legrand Sabin, *Kit Carson Days, 1809–1868* (McClurg, 1914), 512.

"half horse and half alligator": Emerson Hough, *The Way to the West: And the Lives of Three Early Americans, Boone-Crockett-Carson* (Grosset & Dunlap, 1903), 162.

"His well-being rests in no man's hands": Theodore Roosevelt, *Ranch Life and the Hunting Trail* (Century Company, 1899), 83.

CHAPTER 6: THE HUNDRED-YEAR WAR AGAINST THE GRIZZLIES

Hugo Glass saga: Win Blevins, *Give Your Heart to the Hawks: A Tribute to the Mountain Men* (Macmillan, 2005), 52–58.

Old Mose saga: Jack Bell, "Conquest of the King of the Grizzlies," in *The Best of Outdoor Life* (Cowles Creative Publishing, 1998), 11–13.

CHAPTER 7: MASTER HUNTER IN THE WHITE HOUSE

"The collections were at first kept in my room": Theodore Roosevelt, *Roosevelt's Writings: Selections from the Writings of Theodore Roosevelt*, ed. Maurice Garland Fulton (Macmillan, 1920), 247.

"as a boy, he filled his house and pockets with spiders": Candice Millard, *The River of Doubt: Theodore Roosevelt's Darkest Journey* (Knopf, 2009), 23.

"fringed and beaded buckskin shirt": Edmund Morris, *The Rise of Theodore Roosevelt* (Random House, 2010), 275.

"He craved once more to be alone with nature": John Burroughs, "Camping with President Roosevelt," *Atlantic Monthly*, May 1906, 591.

"apparently pathological extremes": Sarah Watts, *Rough Rider in the White House: Theodore Roosevelt and the Politics of Desire* (University of Chicago Press, 2003), 127.

"I owe more than I can ever express": Ibid., 105.

"I have been fulfilling a boyish ambition": Ibid., 105.

"We had found where he had been feeding": Theodore Roosevelt, *The Selected Letters of Theodore Roosevelt*, ed. H. W. Brands (Cooper Square Press, 2001), 40.

"There are no words that can tell": H. W. Brands, *T.R.: The Last Romantic* (Basic Books, 1998), 647.

"I heard him utter a peculiar, savage kind": Theodore Roosevelt, *Hunting Adventures in the West* (G. Putnam's Sons, 1927), 241.

"Instantly the great bear turned": Ray Stannard Baker, "Theodore Roosevelt: A Character Sketch," *McClure's Magazine*, November 1898, 28.

"I leaped to one side": Henry Beach Needham, "Theodore Roosevelt—An Outdoor Man," *McClure's Magazine*, January 1906, 248.

"Before he could get quite all the way round": Theodore Roosevelt, *African Game Trails: An Account of the African Wanderings of an American Hunter-naturalist*, volume 1 (C. Scribner, 1910), 106.

"There have been few days of my hunting life": Theodore Roosevelt, *Hunting Trips of a Ranchman; Hunting Trips on the Prairie and in the Mountains* (Review of Reviews Publishing Company, 1885), 294.

"In trotting, the head and tail": Theodore Roosevelt, *Outdoor Pastimes of an American Hunter* (C. Scribner's Sons, 1905), 204.

"The lumbering, self-confident gait": Roosevelt, *Hunting Trips of a Ranchman*, 133.

"No one, but he who has partaken": Roosevelt, *The Wilderness Hunter*, 11, 12.

"Elk offer easy marks": Roosevelt, *Hunting Trips of a Ranchman*, 304.

"It is four days since we reached the country": Richard Rattenbury, *Hunting the American West: The Pursuit of Big Game for Life, Profit, and Sport, 1800–1900* (Boone and Crockett Club, 2008), 81. This book is an excellent source for background on the history of American hunting.

"In a civilized and cultivated country": Roosevelt, *Outdoor Pastimes of an American Hunter*, 272.

Roosevelt's account of Louisiana hunt: Theodore Roosevelt, "In the Louisiana Canebrakes," *Scribner's Magazine*, January–June 1908.

"Anyone can kill a deer": J. Frank Dobie, *The Ben Lilly Legend* (University of Texas Press, 1981), 55; "I am sure I improve": Ibid., 91.

CHAPTER 8: THE HUNT THAT WENT OUT OF CONTROL

Account of Frank Mayer's hunting: Frank H. Mayer with Charles B. Roth, *The Buffalo Harvest*: http://www.pbs.org/weta/thewest/resources

/archives/five/buffalo.htm, "Buffalo Hunting," *Harper's Weekly*, December 14, 1867.

"It would seem to be hardly possible": Theodore R. Davis, "The Buffalo Range," *Harper's New Monthly Magazine*, December 1868, 149.

"I have done some of the most remarkable shooting": Jim Merritt, "Custer Goes Hunting," *Field & Stream*, July 1999, 65.

"I can take the head and neck of an antelope": Elizabeth Bacon Custer, *Boots and Saddles: Or, Life in Dakota with General Custer* (Harper & Brothers, 1899), 293.

"These men have done more in the last two years": Mari Sandoz and Michael Punke, *The Buffalo Hunters: The Story of the Hide Men* (University of Nevada Press, 2008) 173.

"he realized to perfection the bold hunter": Don Russell, *The Lives and Legends of Buffalo Bill* (University of Oklahoma Press, 1960), 171.

Account of Buffalo Bill's hunt with Alexis: Buffalo Bill and William Lightfoot Visscher, *Buffalo Bill's Own Story of His Life and Deeds: This Autobiography Tells in His Own Graphic Words the Wonderful Story of His Heroic Career* (Homewood Press, 1917), 237–42; and William F. Cody and William Lightfoot Visscher, *The Life and Adventures of Buffalo Bill* (Stanton and Van Vliet, 1917), 234–42.

"Suddenly a cloud of dust rose": Philip St. George Cooke, "Scenes in the West; or, A Night on the Santa Fe Trail, No. III," *Southern Literary Messenger*, February 1842.

"We took away their country": US War Department, *Annual Report of the Secretary of War, 1878*, volume 1, 36.

CHAPTER 9: THE RISE OF THE WOMEN HUNTERS

"I love army life here in the West": Frances Marie Antoinette Mack Roe, *Letters from an Officer's Wife: 1871–1888* (D. Appleton, 1909), 333.

Description of Ella Bird's life: Richard Rattenbury, *Hunting the American*

West: The Pursuit of Big Game for Life, Profit, and Sport, 1800–1900 (Boone and Crockett Club, 2008), 299–301, 305–309, and Ella Elgar Bird Dumont, *An Autobiography of a West Texas Pioneer* (University of Texas Press, 1988), 22–54.

"The bear turned and started back": Grace Gallatin Seton-Thompson, *A Woman Tenderfoot* (Doubleday, Page and Company, 1900), 143.

Wallihan account: Shannan Koucherik, "Moffat County History: Augusta Wallihan—a Lady of the West," *Craig Daily Press* (Colorado), January 31, 2009.

"To say I was overjoyed": Daniel Justin Herman, "The Hunter's Aim: The Cultural Politics of American Sport Hunters, 1880–1910," *Journal of Leisure Research*, Fall 2003.

Longoria details: Eva Longoria, interview on *The Late Show with David Letterman*, January 31, 2008.

Lambert details: Stephen Betts, "Miranda Lambert: Gun Control Debate Won't Draw Singer into Political Firestorm," TheBoot.com, April 25, 2013; Jon Bream, "Don't Mess with Miranda Lambert," *Star Tribune* (Minneapolis), February 23, 2008; J. Freedom du Lac, "Texas Wrangler," *Washington Post*, May 15, 2007; Miranda Lambert Twitter feed posting, November 18, 2012

Lawrence details: Josh Eells, "America's Kick-Ass Sweetheart," *Rolling Stone*, April 12, 2012.

"They don't understand": *Nightline*, ABC News, February 3, 2015.

"I believe with every part of me": *Fox & Friends,* November 17, 2014.

"The number of women I meet": Michael Shea, "Eva Shockey on the Future of Hunting," *Field & Stream*, May 2014.

"Women are realizing how much fun": Kristen A. Schmitt, "More Women Give Hunting a Shot," *National Geographic*, November 4, 2013.

Thompson, McMillen quotes: Richard Grant, "Hunting Is for Girls," Al Jazeera America, February 1, 2015.

CHAPTER 10: AMERICA'S HUNTERS IN CHIEF

"Our heroes were hunters": Don Sapatkin, "American Presidents Often Drawn to Hunting," *Fort Wayne News-Sentinel*, April 28, 2004.

"never much improved afterwards": Abraham Lincoln, *Selections from the Writings of Abraham Lincoln,* ed. Joseph Grégoire de Roulhac Hamilton (Scott, Foresman, 1922), 31.

Lincoln as rifle-technology buff: Carl Sandburg, *Abraham Lincoln: The Prairie Years and the War Years* (Delacorte, 2007), 22; Alexander Rose, *American Rifle: A Biography* (Delacorte, 2009), 143, and William Osborn Stoddard, *Inside the White House in War Times* (C. L. Webster & Co., 1890), 41–44; Alexander Rose, "Lincoln's Rifles," *American Rifleman*, September 15, 2009.

"He loved it for every reason": "Presidents as Sportsmen," *New York Times*, September 11, 1892.

Chester Arthur in Yellowstone: Frank H. Goodyear, *A President in Yellowstone: The F. Jay Haynes Photographic Album of Chester Arthur's 1883 Expedition* (University of Oklahoma Press, 2013).

Cleveland on hunting: Grover Cleveland, *Fishing and Shooting Sketches* (Outing Publishing, 1906), 3, 4, 6–8, 199.

"happiest when he is down on the Chesapeake": "Presidents as Sportsmen."

Harrison as hunter: Miller Center of Public Affairs, University of Virginia, "Benjamin Harrison: Life in Brief," http://millercenter.org /president/bharrison/essays/biography/print; Charles Herr, "Benjamin Harrison's 1895 Fulton Chain Vacation," Adirondack Almanack, February 4, 2014, http://www.adirondackalmanack.com/2014/02 /benjamin-harrisons-1895-fulton-chain-vacation.html#sthash .Cqvns9EY.dpuf.

Coolidge as hunter: Carthon Davis, "Coolidge in Virginia, Thanksgiving 1928," Calvin Coolidge Presidential Foundation website, https:// coolidgefoundation.org/resources/essays-papers-addresses-12/.

FDR as hunter: Sally Denton, *The Plots Against the President: FDR, a Nation in Crisis, and the Rise of the American Right* (Bloomsbury, 2012), 6; William Leuchtenburg, *The White House Looks South: Franklin D. Roosevelt, Harry S. Truman, Lyndon B. Johnson* (LSU Press, 2005), 38; Waldo W. Braden, "Franklin D. Roosevelt Visits Louisiana," *Louisiana History: The Journal of the Louisiana Historical Association*, Autumn 1967, 379–83.

Eisenhower as hunter: Stephen Ambrose, *The Supreme Commander: The War Years of General Dwight D. Eisenhower* (Anchor Books, 2012), 293; Stephen E. Ambrose, *Eisenhower: Soldier and President* (Simon & Schuster, 2014), 29; Carlo D'Este, *Eisenhower: A Soldier's Life* (Macmillan, 2003), 25.

JFK and LBJ as hunters: Brad Bucholz, "The Heart and Soul of LBJ," *Austin-American Statesman*, September 3, 2008; Michael Beschloss, "Kennedy, L.B.J. and a Disputed Deer Hunt," *New York Times*, August 15, 2014.

"I had a fishing pole in my hands": Jimmy Carter, *An Hour Before Daylight: Memories of a Rural Boyhood* (Simon & Schuster, 2001), 97.

"I have used weapons since I was big enough": Jimmy Carter, "What Happened to the Ban on Assault Weapons?" *New York Times*, April 26, 2009.

"Looking back on my hunting days": Jimmy Carter, *An Outdoor Journal: Adventures and Reflections* (University of Arkansas Press, 1994), 51.

"I can still remember the first day": Remarks on Signing Handgun Control Legislation, November 30, 1993, *Public Papers of the Presidents*.

"The joy of fishing with your son": President's News Conference in Pinedale, Wyoming, July 16, 1992, *Public Papers of the Presidents*.

"These aren't animals": United Press International, "Shoot Clay Pigeons, Animal Lovers Tell Bush," December 28, 1988.

"seem like a pretty fun bunch": Zeke Miller, "Obama: Duck Dynasty

Family Seems Like a Pretty Fun Bunch," *Time* online, December 19, 2013.

Obama on guns and hunting: Franklin Foer and Chris Hughes, "Barack Obama Is Not Pleased," *New Republic*, January 27, 2013.

"There is much mystic nonsense": Ernest Hemingway, *True at First Light: A Fictional Memoir* (Simon & Schuster, 2014), 156.

Hemingway's weapons: Silvio Calabi, Steve Helsley, and Roger Sanger, *Hemingway's Guns: The Sporting Arms of Ernest Hemingway* (Down East Books, 2010).

"from thirty-five years of [their] being together": Hemingway, *True at First Light*, 240.

"Mary rented a shooting gallery": Valerie Hemingway, *Running with the Bulls: My Years with the Hemingways* (Random House, 2007), 40.

CHAPTER 11: AMERICAN HUNTING TODAY

"We get ground meat and roasts"; "I always tell my hunters": Bryan Brasher, "Hunters for Hungry Helping Feed Mid-South," *Commercial Appeal* (Memphis), December 24, 2011.

"We're a hunter's paradise"; "My family and I firmly believe": Gillian Graham, "Final Destination for Poached Meat in Maine: Plates of the Poor," *Portland Press Herald*, January 19, 2015.

"We have always been game for game"; "I've been donating venison": Josh Baugh, "Venison from Ranches, Hunters Feeds the Hungry," *Houston Chronicle*, December 29, 2013.

"Over the last 75 years, hunters and recreational shooters": National Shooting Sports Foundation in partnership with the Association of Fish and Wildlife Agencies, "Hunting in America: An Economic Force for Conservation," fact sheet, 2012.

Zuckerberg as hunter: Patricia Sellers, "Mark Zuckerberg's new challenge: Eating only what he kills (and yes, we do mean literally . . .)," *Fortune*,

May 26, 2011 (which reprinted an e-mail from Zuckerberg explaining his personal challenge to eat only those animals he killed), and Patricia Sellers, "Facebook CEO Zuckerberg goes hunting for bison," *Fortune*, September 27, 2011.

CHAPTER 12: VOICES FROM THE HEART OF AMERICAN HUNTING

"Hunting is not merely taking an animal's life": Mary Cabela, e-mail message to the authors.

"If most hunters are like me, they began hunting": David Cabela, communication to the authors.

"Hunting combines an inherent passion": Mark Morgan, *A View from Blind and Field: A Book About Hunting, Friendship and Life* (Hypernicon Group, 2012), cited in http://www.blind-and-field.com/author -bio/.

"Through hunting, we test our bodies": Conservation Force, "The Role and Value of Hunting."

"It has always seemed to me that any man": Archibald Rutledge, *Hunting and Home in the Southern Heartland: The Best of Archibald Rutledge*, ed. James A. Casada (University of South Carolina Press, 1992), 30.

"If you have learned nothing else from hunting": Archibald Rutledge, *An American Hunter* (Stokes, 1937), 149.

"Hunting is one of those pleasures": Ron Spomer, "Why Hunt," *Wildlife Art News*, September/October 1990.

"The essence of being a really good hunter": Hugh Fosburgh, *One Man's Pleasure: A Journal of the Wilderness World* (William Morrow, 1960), 151.

"Modern man desperately needs to get in touch": Nelson Bryant, *Fresh Air, Bright Water: Adventures in Wood, Field, and Stream* (American Heritage Press, 1971), x.

"Animals have consciousness and spirit": Ted Kerasote, "The New Hunter," *Sports Afield*, November 1, 1998.

"The thrill in caribou hunting": Jerome B. Robinson, "Caribou Culture," *Field & Stream*, January 1995, 53.

"We are the biggest conservationists in the world": Fox Business Network, April 29, 2015.

"A sportsman may have hunted deer": Conservation Force, "Kinds of Hunting," http://www.conservationforce.org/rolekinds.html.

"To most of us, hunting": Creative Publishing Editors, *Whitetail Techniques & Tactics* (Creative Publishing International, 2001), 5.

"If hunting is an ancient, obsolete": Richard K. Nelson, *Heart and Blood: Living with Deer in America* (Vintage, 1998), 327.

"If someone who has never owned a gun": Austin D. Haight, *The Biography of a Sportsman* (Crowell, 1939), 206.

"The old man used to say that the best part of hunting": Robert Ruark, *The Old Man and the Boy* (1957; repr. Stackpole, 1989), 205.

"When I was young, I was a hunter": Pete Dunne, "Before the Echo," in David Petersen and Richard A. Nelson, *A Hunter's Heart: Honest Essays on Blood Sport* (Macmillan, 1997), 30.

"While hunting, I've cried": Steven Rinella, *Meat Eater: Adventures from the Life of an American Hunter* (Spiegel & Grau, 2013), 230.

"Life in the open is one of my finest rewards": Dick Lattimer, *I Remember Papa Bear: The Untold Story of the Legendary Fred Bear Including His Secrets of Hunting* (Gun Digest Books, 2006), 85.

"Others around me may opt to eat only plants": M. R. James, "Dealing with Death," in Petersen and Nelson, *A Hunter's Heart*, 107.

"There are those who say the kill": Robert Elman, *Seasons of the Hunter* (Knopf, 1985), 55.

"I did not mind killing anything": Ernest Hemingway, *Green Hills of Africa* (Scribner, 1963), 272.

"A particular virtue of wildlife ethics": Joseph Cea, "Hunting Quotes," *Albany Times-Union* blog, November 28, 2010.

"I do not hunt for the joy of killing": John Madson, Michael McIntosh, and Dycie Madson, *Out Home* (University of Iowa Press, 2008), 7.

"Some people ask why men go hunting": Joseph Cea, "Hunting Quotes," *Times Union* (Albany, NY), http://blog.timesunion.com, November 28, 2010.

ACKNOWLEDGMENTS

We thank John Howard, Mel Berger, our families, and the team at Simon & Schuster and Howard Books, including Philis Boultinghouse and Amanda Demastus.

ABOUT THE AUTHORS

Willie Robertson stars in A&E®'s hit show *Duck Dynasty*® and is the CEO of Duck Commander, a family-operated business that creates products for duck hunters, including duck calls, clothes, and videos.

Willie, along with his wife and business partner, Korie Robertson, also owns and operates Buck Commander, where they create products for deer hunters. Willie took the family duck-call-making company from a living room operation to a multimillion-dollar business. He lives with Korie and their four children, John Luke, Sadie, Will, and Bella, in West Monroe, Louisiana.

———

William Doyle is a *New York Times* bestselling author based in New York. He is coproducer of the hit 2014 PBS special *Navy Seals: Their Untold Story* and coauthor of the companion book. He coauthored Chris Kyle's *American Gun: A History of the U.S. in Ten Firearms*, and his books include *An American Insurrection: James Meredith and the Battle of Oxford, Mississippi, 1962*; *A Soldier's Dream: Captain Travis Patriquin and the Awakening of Iraq*; and *A Mission from God* (with James Meredith).